# BARRON'S BOOK NOTES

# MARK TWAIN'S

# *Tom Sawyer*

BY

Eric F. Oatman
Editor, *Scholastic Update*
Scholastic Inc.

SERIES COORDINATOR

**Murray Bromberg**
Principal, Wang High School of Queens
Holliswood, New York

Past President
High School Principals Association of New York City

BARRON'S EDUCATIONAL SERIES, INC.

*All inquiries should be addressed to:*
**Barron's Educational Series, Inc.**
**250 Wireless Boulevard**
**Hauppauge, New York 11788**

*Library of Congress Catalog Card No. 85-3925*

International Standard Book No. 0-8120-3547-X

**Library of Congress Cataloging in Publication Data**
Oatman, Eric F.
  Mark Twain's Tom Sawyer.

  (Barron's book notes)
  Bibliography: p. 116
  Summary: A guide to reading "Tom Sawyer" with a
critical and appreciative mind encouraging analysis
of plot, style, form, and structure. Also includes
background on the author's life and times, sample tests,
term paper suggestions, and a reading list.
  1. Twain, Mark, 1835–1910. Tom Sawyer. [1. Twain,
Mark, 1835–1910. Tom Sawyer.  2. American Literature—
History and criticism]  I. Title.  II. Series.
PS1306.O28 1985      813'.4      85-3925
ISBN 0-8120-3547-X

PRINTED IN THE UNITED STATES OF AMERICA

567    550    98765432

# CONTENTS

# ADVISORY BOARD

We wish to thank the following educators who helped us focus our *Book Notes* series to meet student needs and critiqued our manuscripts to provide quality materials.

Sandra Dunn, English Teacher
Hempstead High School, Hempstead, New York

Lawrence J. Epstein, Associate Professor of English
Suffolk County Community College, Selden, New York

Leonard Gardner, Lecturer, English Department
State University of New York at Stony Brook

Beverly A. Haley, Member, Advisory Committee
National Council of Teachers of English Student
Guide Series, Fort Morgan, Colorado

Elaine C. Johnson, English Teacher
Tamalpais Union High School District
Mill Valley, California

Marvin J. LaHood, Professor of English
State University of New York College at Buffalo

Robert Lecker, Associate Professor of English
McGill University, Montréal, Québec, Canada

David E. Manly, Professor of Educational Studies
State University of New York College at Geneseo

Bruce Miller, Associate Professor of Education
State University of New York at Buffalo

Frank O'Hare, Professor of English
Ohio State University, Columbus, Ohio

Faith Z. Schullstrom, Member, Executive Committee
National Council of Teachers of English
Director of Curriculum and Instruction
Guilderland Central School District, New York

Mattie C. Williams, Director, Bureau of Language Arts
Chicago Public Schools, Chicago, Illinois

# HOW TO USE THIS BOOK

You have to know how to approach literature in order to get the most out of it. This *Barron's Book Notes* volume follows a plan based on methods used by some of the best students to read a work of literature.

Begin with the guide's section on the author's life and times. As you read, try to form a clear picture of the author's personality, circumstances, and motives for writing the work. This background usually will make it easier for you to hear the author's tone of voice, and follow where the author is heading.

Then go over the rest of the introductory material—such sections as those on the plot, characters, setting, themes, and style of the work. Underline, or write down in your notebook, particular things to watch for, such as contrasts between characters and repeated literary devices. At this point, you may want to develop a system of symbols to use in marking your text as you read. (Of course, you should only mark up a book you own, not one that belongs to another person or a school.) Perhaps you will want to use a different letter for each character's name, a different number for each major theme of the book, a different color for each important symbol or literary device. Be prepared to mark up the pages of your book as you read. Put your marks in the margins so you can find them again easily.

Now comes the moment you've been waiting for—the time to start reading the work of literature. You may want to put aside your *Barron's Book Notes* volume until you've read the work all the way through. Or you may want to alternate, reading the *Book Notes* analysis of each section as soon as you have finished reading the corresponding part of the original. Before you move on, reread crucial passages you don't fully understand. (Don't take this guide's analysis for granted—make up your own mind as to what the work means.)

Once you've finished the whole work of literature, you may want to review it right away, so you can firm up your ideas about what it means. You may want to leaf through the book concentrating on passages you marked in reference to one character or one theme. This is also a good time to reread the *Book Notes* introductory material, which pulls together insights on specific topics.

When it comes time to prepare for a test or to write a paper, you'll already have formed ideas about the work. You'll be able to go back through it, refreshing your memory as to the author's exact words and perspective, so that you can support your opinions with evidence drawn straight from the work. Patterns will emerge, and ideas will fall into place; your essay question or term paper will almost write itself. Give yourself a dry run with one of the sample tests in the guide. These tests present both multiple-choice and essay questions. An accompanying section gives answers to the multiple-choice questions as well as suggestions for writing the essays. If you have to select a term paper topic, you may choose one from the list of suggestions in this book. This guide also provides you with a reading list, to help you when you start research for a term paper, and a selection of provocative comments by critics, to spark your thinking before you write.

# THE AUTHOR AND HIS TIMES

Mark Twain's life illustrates a point he makes in *The Adventures of Tom Sawyer*—that there is no single, simple formula for success. A school dropout at eleven, he spent twenty years in a variety of jobs. He was a typesetter, but, by his own admission, not a very good one. He piloted riverboats, but the Civil War put him out of work. He tried soldiering—and deserted. He spent a disastrous year mining gold and silver.

In desperation, he became a newspaper reporter in Nevada. Running afoul of the law, he fled to San Francisco, found another newspaper job—and got fired.

Twain was thirty now, and about this time he sat in his room, pointed a gun at his head, and contemplated pulling the trigger. It was a good thing he held back. For he soon discovered that he had a talent for "literature," as he wrote his brother, "of a low order—i.e., humorous." Over the next two decades, he wrote several books, which made him rich and world famous. Among those books were two of America's most important contributions to world literature: *The Adventures of Tom Sawyer* and *The Adventures of Huckleberry Finn*.

Surely this is the type of startling reversal worthy of Tom Sawyer—the boy who breaks every rule imaginable, longs for a romantic death, and ends up a rich and revered member of his community. How did Twain manage this feat? For an answer, you should take a close look at the man, his art, and the times in which he lived.

Twain was born on November 30, 1835, in the frontier hamlet of Florida, Missouri. His parents named the sickly child, their fifth, Samuel Langhorne Clemens. (He adopted the pen name Mark Twain in 1863.)

In 1839, John Clemens moved his family from their poor, two-room shack in Florida to Hannibal, Missouri, on the banks of the Mississippi River. Hannibal boasted only 450 citizens when they arrived, but the town seemed destined to thrive and raise the Clemens family's fortunes with it.

Hannibal grew, but the Clemenses did not prosper. Although John Clemens became one of the town's most respected citizens, he went bankrupt, lost all his property in Hannibal, and died of pneumonia in 1847. Samuel was eleven at the time of his father's death. His mother, Jane Clemens, took him into the room where his father's coffin lay and made him promise to behave.

"I will promise anything," Twain would remember saying, "if you don't make me go to school! Anything!"

"No Sammy; you need not go to school anymore. Only promise to be a better boy," his mother said. "Promise not to break my heart."

You will hear echoes of Jane Clemens in *Tom Sawyer*. Twain modeled Tom's Aunt Polly after his mother, whom he called his "first and closest friend." Aunt Polly is not Jane Clemens with a different name and a frontier dialect, however. Jane Clemens was stronger and quicker than Polly. When defending the oppressed, Twain would remember, she was "the most eloquent person I have heard speak."

For two years after his father's death, Samuel worked as an apprentice to a Hannibal printer. In 1850 his older brother, Orion, bought a local newspaper. Samuel went to work for him, but Orion ran such an unprofitable operation that Samuel often went without pay.

In 1853, at age seventeen, Samuel set off on his own. For two years he worked as a typesetter in St. Louis, New York, and Philadelphia before returning to the Mississippi Valley and working once more for Orion, who was now a printer in Keokuk, Iowa.

At this point, Samuel had published several short pieces in Orion's newspaper and a humorous sketch in a Boston magazine. Yet he had no desire to make writing his life's work. He left Keokuk in November 1856, and in the spring he persuaded a steamboat pilot on the Mississippi River to teach him his trade. He spent the next few years steering steamboats up and down the Mississippi. In April 1861, the Civil War halted river traffic between the North and South and put Clemens out of work.

Clemens was unhappy to leave the river. He loved the work and its high pay. Besides, as he wrote in 1875, "A pilot, in those days, was the only unfettered and entirely independent human being that lived in the earth . . . ."

In Chapter 6 of *Tom Sawyer*, Twain speaks of Huck Finn in similar terms. "Huckleberry came and went, at his own free will . . . he did not have to go to school or to church, or call any being master or obey anybody . . . ."

In Iowa, Samuel's brother Orion had backed Abraham Lincoln's 1860 race for the U.S. presidency. His reward was an appointment to a high administrative post in the Nevada Territory. He went with Orion and spent a year unsuccessfully prospecting for gold and silver in Nevada. Broke, he took a job writing for the *Territorial Enterprise* in Virginia City, where for the first time he began signing his pieces "Mark Twain"—the river call for a depth of two fathoms.

Precisely how he chose that name is a mystery. Clemens said he "confiscated" it from a newspaperman who wrote for the *New Orleans Picayune* in the 1850s. However, scholars can find no record of any writer's using that name before Clemens. In Virginia City, Clemens used the river term in a unique way. He would tell bartenders to "mark twain"—that is, to add two more drinks to his bill. Scholars believe it's likely he invented the New Orleans journalist story to disguise his pen name's link to the barroom after he became "respectable" in the East.

After fleeing to California and losing his newspaper job there, Twain wrote sketches for a humor magazine. He published a tall tale in a New York magazine in late 1865. The story—"The Celebrated Jumping Frog of Calaveras County"—was reprinted in newspapers all over the country, and marked the true start of Twain's writing career.

In January 1867, he went to New York City to write a series of travel letters for a California newspaper. He continued writing dispatches for the newspaper after he joined a group of wealthy tourists bound for Europe and the Holy Land.

The trip took five months and had two important consequences for Twain. First, it provided him with material for a book, *The Innocents Abroad*, which brought him fame when it was published in 1869. Second, the trip led to his meeting Olivia ("Livy") Langdon, who would become his wife. Livy's brother had gone on the trip and introduced Twain to his sister afterwards. Twain and Livy were married in February 1870 and went to live in Buffalo, New York. Some scholars believe that Twain's description of Tom and Becky's courtship in *Tom Sawyer* is a parody (take-off) of his own bumpy courtship of Livy.

The couple moved to Hartford, Connecticut , in 1871. There Twain wrote *Roughing It*, a book about his experiences in Nevada and California. Published in 1872, the book added to his reputation as a humorist.

In 1873, he collaborated with a neighbor, Charles Dudley Warner, on his first novel. Called *The Gilded Age*, the novel satirized the political corruption and the mania for speculation that characterized the post Civil War era. The book earned Twain a great deal of money. In 1874 he built his family an extravagant home in Hartford.

Before moving into the home, the family spent the summer in Livy's hometown of Elmira, New York, where Twain began working in earnest on *The Adventures of Tom Sawyer*. He had actually begun the book during the winter of 1872–73, in Hartford, but had put it aside to work on *The Gilded Age*. Now, in Elmira from April to September 1874, he was able to work almost daily on the project. Soon the writing became forced and artificial. "I had worked myself out, pumped myself dry," he wrote a friend. So he put the manuscript aside and wrote a series of articles on his steamboating days, "Old Times on the Mississippi." It wasn't until eight months later that he returned to *Tom Sawyer*.

When the book was finally published in December 1876, the reviews were favorable. Sales, however, were another matter. A Canadian publisher undercut the U.S. edition by flooding the country with a cheap pirated version. Twain's own publisher sold fewer than 27,000 copies of the novel during the first year. Oddly, sales of *Tom Sawyer* never really took off until after 1885, when *The Adventures of Huckleberry Finn* appeared and reviewers began to link the two books in the public's mind. Since then, Americans have bought millions of copies of the novel. It is a favorite of both children and adults—a testament to Twain's genius for enriching his tales of childhood with humor and penetrating insights into human nature.

Most readers agree that *Tom Sawyer* is Twain's second-best book. First-place honors must go to *Huckleberry Finn*, where Twain explores both language and ideas in greater depth. However, *Tom Sawyer* is probably Twain's best-*loved* novel, and its extraordinary success with people of all ages seems to prove it.

To understand *Tom Sawyer*, it may help to put yourself in Twain's place—that of a worldly man, nearing forty, who is viewing childhood across the bridge of thirty years. Between Twain and his boyhood stand years of personal travel, trial, and error; a civil war marked with heroism and sacrifice but also greed and cruelty; an end to slavery; and startling developments in industry and communications. From the vantage point of the post Civil War era, the 1840s must have seemed idyllic indeed—as carefree and innocent as an endless summer.

Primarily, *Tom Sawyer* is a reminiscence of Twain's boyhood, which he recalls with a longing for the past. But it is more than a remembrance because Twain has let his broad literary background shape his memories.

Literary sources for *Tom Sawyer* include Charles Dickens' *A Tale of Two Cities*, which contains a grave-robbing scene like the one Tom and Huck witness. The treasure hunt contains elements of Edgar Allan Poe's story, "The Gold Bug." Although in 1869 Twain claimed to dislike Thomas Bailey Aldrich's *The Story of a Bad Boy*, many readers feel that he borrowed ideas from that book, as well.

Thus, you shouldn't read *Tom Sawyer* as Twain's autobiography. In fact, you even have to read Twain's real autobiography with a grain of salt, for as he warns at the end of one chapter: "Now then, that is the tale. Some of it is true."

The Hannibal of Twain's youth was a far rougher and shabbier place than St. Petersburg, Twain's fictional version of his hometown. A village on the American frontier, Hannibal had a darker side, which Twain only hints at. As a boy, he nearly drowned three times. He watched villagers try—unsuccessfully—to hang an anti-slavery man. He witnessed a hanging, and he watched a man burn to death in a jail cell. He also saw two drownings, an attempted rape, as well as two attempted and four actual murders.

Such experiences helped Twain to understand that life is not a continuous holiday—even for children. Tom's nightmares are one indication of that, as are Twain's angry asides about the villagers' hypocrisies.

Twain doesn't dwell on life's darker side in this novel, however. He wanted to write a light-hearted, entertaining book. Yet woven through it are a number of themes that link it to Twain's later, more philosophical works. (See "Themes," page 20.)

As he grew older, Twain began to examine the less appealing aspects of human nature more relentlessly. *The Adventures of Huckleberry Finn* (1885) is peopled with all types of evil, stupid, or mean characters. *The Tragedy of Pudd'nhead Wilson* (1894), for all its humor, concerns man's corruptness.

The year *Pudd'nhead Wilson* was published, business reverses forced Twain into bankruptcy. He embarked on a world tour, lecturing for $1,000 a night. The success of that tour and of *Following the Equator*, the travel book that came out of it, enabled him to pay his debts.

As he moved toward the end of his life, Twain shed his comic mask and confronted themes of evil and dishonesty with increasing bitterness. This bitterness is evident in such works as "The Man That Corrupted Hadleyburg," a story, and the nonfiction tract, *What Is Man?*

Gnawing financial difficulties and family sorrows were partly responsible for his emphasis on the bleak. His favorite daughter, Susy, died in 1896, his wife in 1904. Another daughter died in 1909. Twain died of heart failure on April 21, 1910, in Redding, Connecticut.

For his readers, Twain lives on—a symbol, like Tom Sawyer, of something raw and unyielding in the American character.

Tom's ability to triumph, whatever the odds, is no doubt a major reason that Twain wrote of him so admiringly. It is surely one reason you will be drawn to Tom, and why you may never forget him.

# THE NOVEL

## The Plot

An orphan named Tom Sawyer lives with his Aunt Polly in St. Petersburg, Missouri, a small town on the banks of the Mississippi River. Tom is not a "model boy," and early one summer around 1845, he proves it. In a single day, he eats jam behind his aunt's back, plays hooky from school and lies to his aunt about it, and fights with a new boy in town.

With helpful hints from Sid, Tom's half-brother, Polly sees through the lie. She punishes Tom by ordering him to whitewash her fence on Saturday. However, Tom finds a way to avoid the work. He makes whitewashing seem like so much fun that other boys give up their prize possessions for the privilege of doing Tom's work.

After playing war games with friends, he notices a new girl in town—Becky Thatcher—who throws him a flower. Smitten, Tom goes home, only to be blamed by Polly for Sid's crime—breaking the sugar bowl.

At Sunday school, Tom trades his whitewashing loot for tickets that boys earned reciting biblical verses. On the way to school the next day, Tom runs into Huckleberry Finn, son of the town drunk, and the two plan a midnight meeting. In school, Tom proposes marriage to Becky, who accepts until she learns that Tom was "engaged" before, to Amy Lawrence. Sulking over his rejection, Tom skips the afternoon session of school and ends up playing Robin Hood with a friend.

After midnight, Tom and Huck walk to the graveyard, where they witness an attempted grave robbery and a murder. Muff Potter and Injun Joe, two drifters, balk at completing the grave robbery until Dr. Robinson, who hired them, doubles their pay. Robinson knocks out Potter, and Injun Joe murders Robinson. Injun Joe shifts the blame for the murder to Potter, a drunk, who is led to believe he might be guilty. Tom and Huck are so frightened of Injun Joe that they pledge never to reveal the truth. After Potter is arrested and jailed, the boys smuggle food and tobacco to his cell but don't tell him they know he is innocent.

Back at school, Becky crushes Tom with another rejection. Tom decides to run away to Jackson's Island, downriver from St. Petersburg. He persuades Huck and another friend, Joe Harper, to join him as "pirates." After midnight, the three steal a raft and head out on their adventure.

The next day they realize that the villagers think they've drowned. While Huck and Joe sleep, Tom returns to St. Petersburg and eavesdrops on a conversation in Polly's house. Tom then returns to the island. Four days later, the boys astonish the villagers by walking in on their own funeral.

At school once more, Tom plays hard-to-get with Becky. She feigns interest in Alfred Temple, who ends up spilling ink on Tom's spelling book. The teacher, however, blames Tom and punishes him. To protect Becky, Tom takes the blame for her accidental tearing of the teacher's anatomy book. This act wins him Becky's love.

Summer passes slowly. Becky has left town. Tom joins and quits a temperance group (dedicated to abstinence from alcohol), catches the measles, and lies in bed for five weeks. After much soul-searching, Tom testifies at Muff Potter's trial and Injun Joe flees. With Injun Joe at large, Tom is terrorized by nightmares.

After a while, Tom ventures out with Huck in search of buried treasure. The boys hide upstairs in a "haunted" house and watch Injun Joe and a sidekick uncover a box of gold coins. Joe takes the box with him, telling his friend he'll hide it in "Number Two—under the cross."

Tom and Huck hunt for the treasure in a local temperance tavern and discover Injun Joe drunk in room No. 2. While Tom is at a picnic hosted by Becky, Huck follows Injun Joe and his sidekick up to the widow Douglas' house on Cardiff Hill. Huck runs for help after learning that Joe plans to avenge an old slight by disfiguring the widow. A Mr. Jones and his two sons rush to the widow's aid, but Injun Joe escapes.

At the picnic, Becky and Tom become lost in an enormous cave. After three days in the cave, during which time Tom spots Injun Joe, Tom manages to become a hero once more by leading Becky to safety. Two weeks later, he learns that Becky's father has sealed the cave with an iron door. Inside the cave, they find Joe, dead of starvation.

Tom and Huck later return to the cave in search of the box of gold coins. They find them and row back to St. Petersburg, intending to hide the coins in Mrs. Douglas' hayloft. But Mr. Jones ushers them into the widow's house, where she is holding a party to thank everyone who helped her against Injun Joe. Tom steals center stage by bringing in the treasure, which amounts to $6000 for each boy.

The boys are now relatively rich. Becky's father has lofty plans for Tom—a military and legal education. Huck lives with the widow, who tries to civilize him. When Huck runs away, Tom persuades him to return by promising him a place in Tom Sawyer's Gang, if Huck becomes "respectable."

# The Characters
## MAJOR CHARACTERS
### Tom Sawyer

Tom, the novel's hero, appears in almost every scene. Poorly behaved, scrappy, and often thoughtless in his pursuit of the spotlight, he triumphs in spite of his bad behavior.

One of Tom's great strengths is his ability to turn everything—from fence-painting to death—into play. He is also a born leader. Again and again, he persuades his friends to do his bidding. Under his command, they become fence painters, soldiers, and English knights. Tom's leadership ability stems in part from his wide reading of romantic literature, which makes him an "expert" on such childhood pleasures as treasure-hunting, pirating, and the lore of Sherwood Forest. Tom also succeeds by trickery. He makes fence-painting seem like so much fun that boys pay him for the right to do it.

Tom is not without qualms, however. His Presbyterian upbringing and his superstitious nature often give him bad dreams and feelings of guilt.

Tom is basically a good boy, in spite of his continual warfare with adults. He apologizes to Polly for embarrassing her. To protect Becky, he takes the blame for the page she tore. He loves his aunt and tells her so—although tardily.

Do you feel, as some readers do, that Tom matures as the novel progresses? Or do you think he simply joins the society whose ways he tested throughout the novel? Perhaps both views are valid—that is, as Tom matures, he realizes how senseless it is to remain, like Huck, at odds with "civilized" society. The novel gives you abundant evidence to support all three views.

Curiously ageless, for most readers Tom stands as a symbol of boyhood on the threshold of the adult world.

## Becky Thatcher

The novel's heroine, Becky Thatcher, is as complex a figure as Tom. Like Tom, her age is not clear—anywhere from nine to thirteen. She has blue eyes and blond hair. As the book begins, she is a newcomer in town, on an extended visit to her uncle. As the book ends, it appears—Twain is unclear on this point—that her family has settled in St. Petersburg. Her father is a judge, well off and highly respected by all citizens. Twain modeled Becky after his first sweetheart, Laura Hawkins.

Becky reflects her upbringing. She is polite, respectful of her elders, and so well-behaved that she has never been whipped in school. Yet in some ways she is no more a "model girl" than Tom is a "model boy." She can be cruel. She feigns interest in Alfred Temple when it enables her to taunt Tom. She can be vindictive. She doesn't stand up for Tom when he's accused of spilling ink on his spelling book because she wants him punished. She can be disobedient. Behind her mother's back, she agrees to Tom's plan to visit Mrs. Douglas' house. She can be a pest. She "teased" her mother to win her consent for the picnic. She has a quick temper, as Tom discovers several times.

Still, Becky is basically warm and considerate.

Lost in the cave, she regains hope in order to make Tom stop blaming himself for their plight. She appreciates Tom's efforts on her behalf and says so, to Tom and her father. Yet she is generally presented as so strong-willed that some readers are startled by the speed with which, at the outset, she gives up hope in the cave. This passive acceptance of fate seems out of character. During Twain's time, however, women were considered the weaker sex, and their characterization in fiction reflected this view.

## Aunt Polly

The sister of Tom's dead mother, Polly is modeled after Twain's mother, Jane Clemens. Twain claimed that, besides having Polly speak in dialect, he couldn't "think up other improvements" for his mother. However, Twain's mother was stubborn, proud, and quick-witted; Polly is none of these. Some readers believe that Polly is partly modeled after Mrs. Partington, a character in one of Twain's favorite books, Benjamin P. Shillaber's *Life and Sayings of Mrs. Partington*. A strict Calvinist, Mrs. Partington nevertheless cannot bear to discipline her orphaned nephew, Ike, who outwits her at every turn. Similarly, Polly believes it her duty to discipline Tom, yet she is too soft-hearted to do it regularly.

## Huckleberry Finn

Huck is in many ways Tom's opposite. Part of St. Petersburg's outcast community—a group that includes slaves, drunks, and criminals—Huck represents all that the village's "respectable" citizens abhor. He is dirty, lazy, uneducated, and the son of a town drunk. He is a follower, not a leader. Untouched by formal religion, he is not harassed by his conscience as Tom is. He puts his own safety first until, near the end of the novel, he aids Mrs. Douglas. The ways of civilization hold no joys for him, as he learns when he becomes "rich" and Mrs. Douglas tries to mold him into a sort of "model boy."

Twain modeled Huck after a boy named Tom Blankenship, someone he remembered as "the only really independent person—boy or man—in the community." But some readers believe Huck's relationship with Tom is based on Twain's reading of Miguel de Cervantes' *Don Quixote de la Mancha*, a seventeenth century burlesque of popular Medieval romances of chivalry. Huck, like Quixote's sidekick, Sancho Panza, is uneducated and matter-of-fact. Twain develops his character more fully in *The Adventures of Huckleberry Finn*, whose popularity caused Huck to overshadow Tom in the public's imagination. Here, however, Huck is clearly subordinate to Tom.

## Sid

Twain uses Tom's half-brother, Sid, to make good boys look bad. Sid stays out of trouble yet never tires of reporting Tom's infractions to Polly. He is sneaky and mean-spirited, gaining attention at the expense of others.

Twain's younger brother, Henry Clemens, served as the model for Sid. However, Twain defended his brother by calling Henry "a very much better and finer boy than Sid ever was."

## Mary

Tom's cousin, Mary, is an even-tempered teenager who is the fourth member of Aunt Polly's household. She is kind to Tom, who likes her. A patient girl, she rewards Tom for his successes instead of scolding him for his mistakes. Mary is thought to be modeled after Pamela Clemens, Twain's sister, who, after their father died, taught piano to help support her family.

## Injun Joe

The only evil character in the novel, Injun Joe is one of St. Petersburg's outcasts. He is of mixed Indian and white parentage, like the man of the same name who lived in Hannibal during Twain's youth, and whose worst crime was getting drunk.

Injun Joe is driven by a desire for revenge. He murders the young Dr. Robinson because Robinson's father had him jailed as a vagrant some years earlier. He wants to disfigure Mrs. Douglas because her late husband, a justice of the peace, had ordered him whipped on the same charge. Some readers see the "murderin' half-breed" as the victim of racial injustice and his actions as a product of that injustice.

Some readers feel that Injun Joe is not a totally believable villain. They see him as a comic book caricature of a villain—more amusing than threatening. Do you agree or disagree?

## Muff Potter

A good-for-nothing, Potter acts kindly toward the boys, sharing his fish with them and fixing their kites. He gets drunk often enough to believe that he might not have remembered killing Dr. Robinson at the graveyard. He seems too mild-mannered to hold a grudge, and he is not at all angry to learn that Tom waited weeks before revealing the evidence that saved him from the gallows.

Potter's real-life counterpart seems to have been Benson, the older brother of Tom Blankenship (the model for Huck). Like Potter, "Bence" Blankenship was treated as an outcast by Hannibal's adults. Many of Hannibal's children, on the other hand, viewed him as a friend.

# MINOR CHARACTERS

## Mrs. Douglas

The widow of St. Petersburg's justice of the peace, she is a hospitable and attractive woman in her early forties. She likes children, and they visit her often. She nurses Huck back from his illness and agrees to take him under her roof. When Huck disappears, she is so distressed that she spends two days hunting for him.

Twain modeled the widow after Mrs. Richard Holliday, a wealthy woman who lived on Holliday's Hill (Cardiff Hill in the novel). As a boy, Twain watched her shoot and kill a man who had gone to her house to assault her.

## Judge Thatcher

Becky's father, a county judge, is highly respected by the villagers, one of whom is St. Petersburg's lawyer Thatcher, Jeff's father. An authoritative figure, he is given the seat of honor when he visits the Sunday school. He leads the search for Becky and Tom and heads the party that discovers Injun Joe dead in the cave.

## Dr. Robinson

A young physician, Robinson makes the fatal mistake of asking Injun Joe—whom he had once refused to feed—to help him rob a grave. His counterpart in Twain's youth was Dr. E.D. McDowell, who ran a medical school in St. Louis and stole corpses for his students to study.

## Mr. Jones

The Welshman who lives with his sons on Cardiff Hill, he rushes to the widow's aid when Huck alerts him. He promises Huck he won't tell who alerted him and remains true to his word. After Injun Joe is found dead, however, he reveals Huck's part in the episode. He is thought to be based on John Davies, a bookseller in Hannibal.

## Mr. Dobbins

The schoolmaster, frustrated in his attempt to become a doctor, is not a happy man. He vents his unhappiness on his students, who avenge themselves on "Examination Night" by having a cat pull off his wig in front of the audience. The schoolmaster in Twain's time was J.B. Dawson, whose son, Theodore, was Hannibal's "model boy."

## Alfred Temple

A newcomer from St. Louis, Temple is a snob who wears shoes on weekdays, while all the other boys go barefoot. He is briefly Tom's rival for Becky's affections. Spurned, he turns into a sneak and pours ink on Tom's spelling book.

## Joe Harper

Tom's best friend, Joe accompanies Tom and Huck to Jackson's Island. He is the first of the three to admit to homesickness.

# Other Elements
## SETTING

*The Adventures of Tom Sawyer* takes place in the "poor little shabby village of St. Petersburg," Missouri, on the banks of the Mississippi River. West of the town lies Cardiff Hill, a "Delectable Land" of fantasy and dreams where Tom loves to play and where the widow Douglas lives. Downriver a few miles, near the Illinois bank, is Jackson's Island, an uninhabited place to which Huck, Tom, and Joe Harper escape for several days of freedom.

St. Petersburg is an idealized version of Hannibal, the Missouri river town where Twain lived as a youngster from 1839 to 1853. This prettified portrayal of the scene of his youth has led many readers to call the novel an *idyll*—a work that paints a scene of country life as one of tranquil happiness.

Yet St. Petersburg is not simply the heavenly place its name suggests. It is a frontier town, literally on the edge of civilization, where anything can happen. The outwardly placid setting is seeded with insincerity, violence, and downright evil.

St. Petersburg, like the Hannibal of Twain's youth, contains people of all types, from all classes. It has the lawyers and drunks, slaves and slaveowners, hypocrites and honest souls. If you appreciate these many distinctions—especially those of social class—you will have a more complete understanding of the novel.

In fact, some readers argue that the novel is one of the first attempts in American literature to portray the social life of a typical American community. Like a tour guide, Twain takes you on a visit to Sunday school, church, an inquest, a funeral, a school's closing exercises, a trial, a picnic, and a party. He also takes you behind the scenes, where you witness a murder, an attempted assault on a widow, a bar masquerading as a non-liquor serving "temperance tavern," as well as multiple hypocrisies. Largely set in motion by adults, most of these forces serve as obstacles to Tom. The novel is in one sense a chronicle of Tom's attempts to overcome them—to survive in spite of the setting's visible perils and those that lurk beneath its surface.

The book takes place simultaneously in a second setting—the world of childhood. This world of innocence and experimentation exists in no specific time frame and no specific physical setting.

# THEMES

Many readers have trouble spotting a central idea or important themes in *The Adventures of Tom Sawyer*. You may agree, noting that, as Twain stated in his preface, one of his main goals was to generate nostalgia—playing off adults' longing for the simpler world of childhood.

On the other hand, a close reading of the novel may suggest several themes to you. Here are some of those themes and evidence to support them.

## 1.   A CHILD'S WORLD IS A DANGEROUS PLACE

Violence is a fact of life in St. Petersburg. Drownings, murders, and other threats to life are commonplace. Tom is haunted by his fear of Injun Joe, whose reputation for violence is such that no villager dares charge him with grave robbery. Tom and Becky narrowly escape starving to death in McDougal's cave. All four plot strands concern death or near death—Dr. Robinson's; the runaway boys'; Becky's and Tom's; and Injun Joe's.

## 2.   A CHILD'S WORLD IS PLAGUED WITH MORAL UNCERTAINTY

Questions of right and wrong are woven through the text. Is Tom right to steal a doughnut when his aunt isn't looking? Should the boys have stolen provisions for their trip to Jackson's Island? What is the right thing for Tom and Huck to do about the murder they witnessed? It is right for Tom to con his friends out of their prized possessions, and then trade them for a Bible he does not deserve?

The characters don't resolve all these (and other) questions, leading one reader to complain of Twain's "moral evasiveness." Yet the characters—especially Tom—are painfully aware of them, as their troubled consciences testify.

### 3. VANITY AND REVENGE MOTIVATE A GOOD DEAL OF HUMAN BEHAVIOR

The novel is full of showoffs—from Aunt Polly, who is mildly vain, to Tom, who strives to be the center of attention. In between these extremes are characters like the fashionable Sunday school superintendent, whose boot toes are bent "like sleigh-runners," and the bewigged schoolmaster, Mr. Dobbins.

As for revenge, this motive stands behind Injun Joe's murder of Dr. Robinson and his attempt to disfigure Mrs. Douglas' face. Revenge motivates Becky's desire to see Tom punished for something he didn't do, and it prompts Tom to hurl clods of dirt at his half-brother, Sid.

### 4. MATERIAL SUCCESS IS THE KEY TO ADMISSION TO RESPECTABLE ADULT SOCIETY

Tom buys temporary success in Sunday school, wins a Bible, and gets to stand near the great Judge Thatcher. After finding the treasure, he and Huck—an outcast for most of the novel—become celebrities and full-fledged members of St. Petersburg society. Some readers even believe that Tom becomes that society's apologist (a person who speaks or writes in defense of a cause).

### 5. CHILDREN AND ADULTS ARE NATURALLY AT ODDS

Tension between adults and children is a recurrent theme that runs through the novel from its first sentences to its last. Adults aim to "civilize" children—something that children, being free spirits, often find intolerable and rebel against. Tom and the adults in his world are in a constant state of war—one in which he tends to win most of the battles. Viewed from an adult perspective, Tom and especially Huck are outlaws for refusing to accept the code of civilized behavior. In their fantasies—as Robin Hood, pirates, and robbers—and in the wilderness of Jackson's Island, they flourish and are happiest.

In the end, however, Tom seems to join the enemy. He takes it upon himself to civilize Huck, the last holdout against the bondage of those values—cleanliness, regularity, scholarship, religious devotion—that society deems desirable.

### 6. SOCIETY ENCOURAGES AND EVEN REWARDS INSINCERITY

Twain exposes insincerity many times in the novel. At the boys' funeral, the minister, with the complicity of the congregation, turns the boys' faults into praiseworthy deeds. On "Examination Night," young ladies demonstrate that they have learned how to tack sermons of "glaring insincerity" onto their compositions.

### 7. "BAD BOYS" CAN TRIUMPH

Tom is the type of person that many children's books used to warn children not to be. Twain turns the message of those books on its head here, creating a hero, rather than a villain, who lies, steals, cheats, and disobeys his elders, yet still ends up healthy, wealthy, and wise.

# STYLE

In *The Adventures of Tom Sawyer*, Twain uses language that is, for the most part, simple, direct, and unpretentious. In most of his sentences, every word has a job. "The old lady pulled her spectacles down and looked over them, about the room," he writes in Chapter 1; "then she put them up and looked out under them." A typical Twain sentence, it describes a comic action—Aunt Polly's glasses were useless—with precision and not a word more than needed. No wonder his spare (lean) style influenced so many writers who followed him, including Ernest Hemingway, who once said that all American literature begins with Mark Twain.

Twain's style in this novel is not consistently spare, however. In places, his style becomes indirect, wordy, and unnecessarily "fancy." Sulking in Chapter 3, Tom "wandered far from the accustomed haunts of boys, and sought desolate places that were in harmony with his spirit. A log raft in the river invited him, and he seated himself on its outer edge and contemplated the dreary vastness of the stream . . . ."

This is one of the many passages that Twain might have simplified but didn't. He probably wanted to mock Tom's romantic posturing by using the type of overblown prose that writers such as James Fenimore Cooper used. However, no such reasoning can explain complicating his prose with such words as "ambuscade" and "adamantine"—both found in one sentence at the end of Chapter 1. Compared with the simple words Twain uses most of the time, these words seem phony, an attempt to sound "literary."

Twain himself preaches against "fine language" and "prized words" in Chapter 21. In general, he heeds his own advice and sticks to simple words and sentences.

Twain's imagery—mostly visual, sometimes auditory and tactile (pertaining to touch)—is never flashy. It is most evident when his attention turns to nature, as on Jackson's Island in Chapter 14. Tom awakens to a "cool gray dawn" (tactile and visual) and observes "beaded dew-drops" (visual) on the leaves. "A white layer of ashes covered the fire, and a thin blue breath of smoke rose straight into the air" (visual). The birds awaken, and "presently [Tom hears] the hammering of a wood-pecker" (auditory).

There's nothing forced about such images. They are as simple and as natural as Twain's informal language. Yet there's a beauty to their simplicity that gives them power. It might be useful to jot down the first ten images that make an impression on you and ask yourself why they are memorable.

Much of the book's humor comes from the several dialects (variations of local speech) that Twain's characters speak. "Hang the boy, can't I never learn anything?" Polly asks herself in Chapter 1. "Ain't he played me tricks enough like that for me to be looking out for him by this time? But old fools is the biggest fools there is."

By recording the way people actually talked on the Missouri frontier, Twain makes his characters both believable and funny. He points up the humor in everyday situations. Such a writer is called a "comic realist"—someone who portrays life humorously but faithfully.

Twain faces the everyday world as a frontier humorist, a writer (or lecturer) who masks his sophistication behind an unassuming "aw-shucks" demeanor. This air of innocence enables Twain to deliver social criticism in an offhanded, almost unintentional way. "A robber is more high-toned than what a pirate is—as a general thing," Tom tells Huck in Chapter 33. "In most countries they're [robbers are] awful high up in the nobility—dukes and such." With a seemingly innocent remark, Twain pokes fun at society's upper crust by suggesting that it is made up of thieves. This aspect of his humor can be seen as, ultimately, subversive.

Twain can evoke terror as well as laughter with his descriptions. You will notice that much of the power of Chapter 31, in which Tom and Becky are lost in the cave, comes from Twain's ability to direct your attention to key details. "Under the roof," he writes, "vast knots of bats had packed themselves together, thousands in a bunch; the lights disturbed the creatures and they came flocking down by hundreds, squeaking and darting furiously at the candles." Twain's simple descriptive style is a flexible tool, and he uses it masterfully to tell his story and guide your reactions to it.

# POINT OF VIEW

*The Adventures of Tom Sawyer* is told by a third-person omniscient (all-knowing) narrator. Some readers believe that Twain made a mistake by writing in the third person. They feel the use of the third person forced him to use a more formal vocabulary than he was comfortable with. As you read *Tom Sawyer*, you might want to ask yourself if a retelling by Tom, in the first person, would have made certain scenes more effective.

The narrator is perhaps Tom's most ardent fan. Some parents might scold their child for conning his friends into doing his work and having them pay for the privilege. Twain doesn't censure Tom for that or for the thoughtless way he hurts Polly's feelings in Chapter 8. Instead, he looks on tolerantly, with a "boys-will-be-boys" attitude that is infectious.

Ordinarily, the narrator lets the material speak for itself. However, a few times he addresses you directly—an occurrence that many readers find jarring.

In all, the narrator is a reliable reporter of the events in St. Petersburg. Yet, St. Petersburg is not Hannibal, the town after which it is modeled, and it would be a mistake to think so. A distance of thirty years allowed Twain to view his hometown—and boyhood—through rose-tinted glasses.

## FORM AND STRUCTURE

The novel's title is a clue to its structure. Rather than a tightly plotted story, it is a series of adventures that Twain has strung together chronologically in thirty-five chapters. The novel's episodic form has led some readers to say that *The Adventures of Tom Sawyer* has no plot at all. However, a close look will show you that four loose plot lines help tie the novel together and give it unity.

The first of these four stories involves Tom's courtship of Becky Thatcher. This plot line begins in Chapter 3 and runs, intermittently, all the way to Chapter 35. The main climax of this story comes in Chapter 32, with the couple's escape from

McDougal's cave. A less important climax occurs in Chapter 20, when Tom wins Becky's heart.

The second story concerns the framing of Muff Potter for Dr. Robinson's murder. This plot line begins in Chapter 9, has its courtroom climax in Chapter 23, and ends in Chapter 24.

The third story concerns the Jackson's Island episode—the boys' running away and their return to witness their own funeral. It begins in Chapter 13, has its climax at the funeral in Chapter 17, and concludes with Chapter 19.

The fourth story traces Injun Joe's fate from the time he flees the courtroom in Chapter 17. The story continues to Chapter 35, where Twain explains how Tom and Huck have been affected by the treasure that Injun Joe found for them. The climax to this plot line occurs in Chapter 33, when the villagers discover Injun Joe's body.

Five chapters (1, 2, 5, 21, and 22) are wholly devoted to adventures that are unrelated to any of the four plot lines. These chapters allow Twain to introduce and develop Tom's character (chapters 1 and 2), describe a church service or a school exercise (chapters 5 and 21), and sum up several weeks in a few pages. By detailing everyday events in these chapters and elsewhere, Twain adds realism to his treatment of life in a Missouri river town before the Civil War.

Readers have pointed to several parallels among the plot lines. For one thing, they all involve deaths—real or imagined. For another, they all end somewhat predictably—two with resurrections, one with a narrow escape from the gallows, and one with a villain's death and the capture of his treasure. Finally, all four stories have the same hero— Tom Sawyer—an orphan who raises himself from near rags to near riches on the strength of his courage and imagination.

# The Story
## DEDICATION

Twain adored his wife, Olivia Langdon Clemens, whom he had married only two years before beginning work on *Tom Sawyer*. She read his books before they were published and often suggested changes.

When Twain finished *Tom Sawyer*, he felt that he had written a book for adults. Olivia and Twain's friend, the novelist and editor William Dean Howells, convinced him otherwise. "Mrs. Clemens decides with you that the book should issue as a book for boys, pure and simple—and so do I," he wrote Howells. "It is surely the correct idea."

## PREFACE

Like the conclusion that Twain tacks onto the end, the preface is an integral part of the novel. Don't skip it. Its three short paragraphs suggest Twain's aim of creating a realistic portrait of small-town life "thirty or forty years ago." Since the novel was published in 1876, this places the action in the 1840s.

The 1840s were idyllic times for Hannibal, the model for St. Petersburg. The little river town of more than a thousand people in the mid-1840s was thriving. The question of allowing Missouri to enter the Union as a slave state had been fiercely debated two decades earlier, with Missouri entering the Union as a slave state in 1821. The upheaval of the Civil War was still a long way off.

Twain says that "most of the adventures recorded in this book really occurred." This statement is largely true, although Twain embellished his adventures with material gleaned from his wide reading, as has been noted in "The Author and His Times" section.

Twain also refers to the superstitions "prevalent in the West" (the Midwest, today) when he was a boy. These superstitions—part of the folklore of his times—fascinated him. He had begun taking notes on them more than ten years before he wrote *Tom Sawyer*.

Finally, Twain tells you exactly for whom the book was written. Always on the lookout for ways to enlarge his readership, Twain describes the book's audience in the broadest terms. It is a book for boys and girls, he says. But, he hopes adults will read it, too, as a reminder of "what they once were themselves, and of how they felt and thought and talked . . . ."

# CHAPTER 1

Approach this chapter as you would another world—one that existed nearly a century and a half before you were born. Try to imagine the people who live there. You meet two of the book's major characters: Tom Sawyer and his Aunt Polly. You also meet two minor characters who act as Tom's "foils"—people who make him look better. One is Sid, Tom's half-brother. The other is a boy with a "citified air" who is a stranger in town.

As Twain opens the book, Aunt Polly is calling her nephew, Tom. The fact that he doesn't answer is a clue to his character: either he isn't where he is supposed to be, or he's just not listening.

---

**NOTE: Twain's use of nostalgia**   Mark Twain took great pride in being able to hold the attention of audiences he lectured to. With this simple opener, he shows he knows how to hook readers too. Tom's situation—being the object of an adult's shout—is one anyone can identify with. Most people can remember, with a mixture of pain and warmth, the emotions they felt when called away from a private task by a familiar parental voice. Twain no doubt knew this. And he probably suspected that Polly's shout would capture the attention of many adults by its appeal to nostalgia—their longing for experiences of the past.

---

From the start, Aunt Polly is a comic figure, but one that Twain portrays warmly. Vain, like other mortals, Polly wears spectacles ror style,' not service." To see, she has to peek over or below them.

Tom doesn't seem to be inside. Polly pokes under the bed with a broom but raises only a cat. Nor is Tom outside in the garden, a tangle of tomato vines and smelly jimson weeds. Only when he tries to sneak by her does Polly realize that he has been hiding in a closet. From the "truck" (rubbish) on his mouth and hands, she knows that he has been helping himself to jam.

Polly decides to flog him, but Tom is too quick for her. "Look behind you, aunt!" he says, and as she does so, he leaps over the fence. This is only the first of many practical jokes he will play on her. Tom's escape makes Polly laugh. His tricks amuse her, though she is troubled that she allows herself to be charmed by him. Tom is her "own dead sister's boy." She accepts the fact that he is full of the "Old Scratch" (the devil), but she feels responsible for his upbringing. Still, she can't bring herself to whip him.

Tom plays hooky from school. He returns home just in time to do his chores—helping a slave boy, Jim, saw wood.

---

**NOTE: Slavery**  Twain calls Hannibal, his boyhood home, St. Petersburg—St. Peter's place, a reference to Heaven. However, it isn't Heaven for everyone, and the appearance of Jim is a clue. Jim—modeled after Sandy, a slave the Clemenses kept in Hannibal—is Polly's slave. As previously mentioned, Missouri was admitted to the Union as a slave state in 1821. Twain dealt with the injustices of slavery in two of his most famous books, *Huckleberry Finn* and *Pudd'nhead Wilson*. However, he almost completely avoids such weighty issues here, in this pleasurable romp through childhood. In any case, you should note the role of such figures as Jim in the novel.

---

At dinner, Polly pumps Tom for clues to his whereabouts during the afternoon. Tom has nearly convinced her that he didn't go swimming when Sid points out that Tom's collar is sewn shut with black thread, although Polly had sewn it with white thread in the morning. (In his *Autobiography*, Twain says that his mother used to sew his shirt tight to keep him from skipping school for a swim.)

Tom darts out the door, vowing to beat up Sid for giving him away. Twain adds a comment, telling you—as if you didn't already know—that Tom "was not the Model Boy of the village." Why does Twain tell you something you already know? First, he's setting up a joke, whose punch line is, "He knew the Model Boy very well though—and loathed him." Second, he's giving you a clue to one of his goals in writing *Tom Sawyer*. By making a "bad boy" a hero, Twain is making fun of books that present boys and girls with perfect behavior as models for their readers.

Tom comes upon a newcomer—a dressed up boy whose "citified air" irks him. It's Friday, and the boy is wearing shoes, something Tom would do only on Sundays. What bothers Tom most is that the boy's clothes make Tom feel "shabbier and shabbier." His first comment to the newcomer is a challenge: "I can lick you!"

The boys fight, and Tom wins. He chases the boy home and waits outside his house until his enemy's mother orders him away. Tom tries to sneak into his own house after dark by climbing through a window. But Polly is waiting for him, determined to punish him.

---

**NOTE: Tom's age**   Twain never specifies Tom's age. Sometimes—as when Polly catches him with jam on his face—he seems no more than eight. Other times, as when he curses his bad luck and wrestles with the overdressed boy, he seems considerably older, maybe twelve or thirteen. Later, he seems even older. Why doesn't Twain keep Tom's actions consistent with those of a particular age group? Some readers see this inconsistency as a flaw. Others dismiss the question by suggesting that Twain is recreating, in the time frame of a few months, all of boyhood—a stage of development that takes years.

## CHAPTER 2

In this chapter, Twain recounts one of the most famous scenes in American literature. Take a few moments after reading the chapter to decide how he makes whitewashing a fence such a memorable experience.

Saturday morning brings Tom's punishment. Aunt Polly has ordered him to whitewash ninety square yards of fence. To make matters worse, the weather is gorgeous. Notice how Twain sets the scene in the opening paragraph. The summer morning is "bright and fresh" and "brimming with life." Cardiff Hill, just north of the village, seems "dreamy" and "inviting."

**NOTE: A "delectable land"**   Twain compares Cardiff Hill to the Delectable Mountains in John Bunyan's religious allegory, *Pilgrim's Progress*, published in 1678. In the mid-19th century most literate Americans were acquainted with *Pilgrim's Progress*, one of the great works of literature, whose symbolic place-names, characters, and action were designed to teach a lesson in Christian moral values. Why do you think Twain introduces this reference to a moral story as a preface to the whitewashing scene?

Tom steps into this blissful scene armed with a

bucket of whitewash and a brush. His depression deepens when he compares his first stroke with the "far-reaching continent of unwhitewashed fence." He sits, moping, on a box built around a tree to protect it.

Jim comes by, and Tom promises to do Jim's chore—fetching water—if Jim helps paint the fence. But Jim won't consider risking Polly's wrath until Tom offers him an alabaster marble—a "white alley." It's a "bully" (slang for *excellent*) "taw," a large, fancy marble normally used for shooting. By relying on these unusual terms, Twain reminds you that the world of childhood has its own language. How does Twain's use of these words help make his story seem true-to-life?

When Tom tops his offer by promising Jim a glimpse of his sore toe, Jim can't resist. But Polly kills the deal by appearing out of nowhere, swatting Jim's rear with a slipper, and sending him on his way and Tom back to work.

Ben Rogers, one of Tom's friends, "hove in sight" (came into view)—a sailor's term that indicates Ben is lost in the fantasy that he is a steamboat. Notice the loving detail with which Twain presents Ben's fantasy. He recreates the tooting of the fog horn and the ding-dong of the ship's bells, the captain's orders, even the motions of the pilot at the wheel.

Tom pretends to be engrossed in his own project. Ben says he is going swimming, but Tom refuses to take the bait. He keeps working as if he enjoys it. Pretty soon, Ben asks if he can "whitewash a little," and Tom consents in exchange for Ben's apple. Other boys come by, and Tom manages to sell them the chance to whitewash the fence too.

By midafternoon, the fence has three coats of

whitewash on it, and Tom is "literally rolling in wealth." For the right to whitewash the fence, St. Petersburg's boys have given him their most valuable possessions.

How did he do it? According to Twain, he discovered "a great law of human action": that you can make people want something by making that something hard to get. Twain—"the writer of this book"—steps into his own story here with a definition of work ("whatever a body is *obliged* to do") and play ("whatever a body is not obliged to do"). The comment doesn't seem out of place because Twain introduces it with irony—saying one thing (that he is "a great and wise philosopher") and meaning another (that he is not a philosopher at all).

What does this chapter teach you about Tom? It's clear that he is a clever actor and a leader. But he is still a child, able to cherish items that adults would consider worthless: a piece of broken glass, a brass doorknob, and a knife handle.

---

**NOTE: The scene as satire**   Some readers feel that Twain satirizes (makes fun of) adult society throughout *Tom Sawyer*. It's an interesting point of view and one that finds support in this scene. Here, some readers feel, Twain uses comedy to ridicule the acquisitive instincts that seemed to rule American society after the Civil War, when Twain wrote the novel. With double-talk, Tom manipulates his friends into doing his work and ends up "rolling in wealth." But the wealth is just things—worthless things, at that.

# CHAPTER 3

This chapter takes the story of Tom's Saturday from late afternoon to bedtime. Its episodic structure—seven episodes strung together—reflects the structure of the entire novel. A close look at the way the episodic pattern works in this chapter will help you understand the way the novel is structured.

**Episode 1:** Tom reports "his" fence-painting success to Aunt Polly, who examines the work to make sure he's telling the truth. When she discovers the job done, she turns a compliment into a lesson: "You *can* work when you're a mind to, Tom." She even delivers his reward—an apple—with a quote from the Bible. This lesson misses its mark, too. As she talks about the value of getting something "without sin through virtuous effort," Tom steals a doughnut.

---

**NOTE: Polly's house** Twain's description of Polly's house is a clue that he is thinking of the house he lived in as a boy in Hannibal. The Clemens house still exists and can be visited, as can the house across the street, which belonged to Elijah Hawkins. The Hawkins house is mentioned later in this chapter as the Thatcher house.

---

**Episode 2:** Outside, Tom settles a score with Sid by clobbering him with clods of dirt. Polly rescues Sid, and Tom leaps the fence, in too much of a hurry to use the gate.

**Episode 3:** Tom and his friend Joe Harper lead

opposing "armies" of boys in a mock battle in the village square. Tom's army wins a "great victory."

---

NOTE: **Tom's generalship**   Whenever Tom is with other boys, he takes a leadership role. Often, as here, the role is a romantic one. What does this tell you about Tom's character? Does he have a need to manipulate others? Or does his love of being in the spotlight as a heroic figure prompt him to devise ways to gain attention?

---

**Episode 4:** Tom passes Jeff Thatcher's house and spots a "lovely little blue-eyed creature with yellow hair." She is Becky Thatcher, although Twain doesn't reveal her name here. Tom is so taken by this pretty stranger that he forgets his former love, Amy Lawrence, and begins showing off in front of Becky. Playing her part in this courting ritual, Becky tosses a pansy to Tom as she disappears into the house. Tom remains in front of her house until nightfall, still showing off.

**Episode 5:** Tom's spirits are so high at supper that his aunt's scolding doesn't faze him. Sid accidentally breaks the sugar bowl, and Tom can't wait to see his good brother punished. Polly assumes Tom broke the bowl, however, and knocks him down.

She is conscience-struck when she realizes she hit the wrong person. Yet as a figure of authority, she can't bring herself to admit she was wrong. Tom, in a sulk, refuses to allow her to make up to him. He fantasizes revenge: lying on his deathbed, he refuses to forgive her; drowned, he does not come to life when Polly begs God to "give her back her boy." These fantasies foreshadow the adventures that will take place in chapters 15 and 17.

---

**NOTE: Emotional insights**    Take a second look at the paragraph that describes Tom's sulking. This wonderful passage shows Twain once more making good use of nostalgia. More importantly, it gives you a chance to appreciate Twain's understanding of human emotions—Tom's and Polly's—and his willingness to indulge Tom's feelings of self-pity. Most children have had the kind of emotional tug-of-war that Tom has with Polly. Most also have fantasies of the "she'll-be-sorry" type. Twain appeals to your sense of nostalgia with his perfect description of Tom's swallowing his tears. But he goes beyond that. He shows Tom actually enjoying his unhappiness.

---

**Episode 6:** Sitting on a raft and wishing he were dead, Tom remembers Becky's flower. He goes to her house, lost in self-pity, and lies beneath her window. He clasps the pansy to his chest as if he were a corpse. Just as he envisions her dropping "one little tear upon his poor lifeless form," a maid opens the window and pours a pitcher of water on him. He runs home.

**Episode 7:** Tom examines his wet clothes by candlelight before going to bed. Sid wakes up and sees Tom but thinks better of saying anything.

## CHAPTER 4

This chapter concerns Sunday school and the preparations for it. The first chapter in which adults play an extensive role, it gives you a chance to compare the children and their elders—and perhaps to discover some resemblances.

Sunday morning begins with breakfast and family worship. The worship consists largely of biblical quotations and "a grim chapter of the Mosaic Law"—codes of conduct, including the Ten Commandments, handed down mainly in the Old Testament by Moses.

---

**NOTE: The novel as idyll**   Many readers describe *Tom Sawyer* as an idyll—a composition in poetry or prose that paints a scene or episode, especially of country life, as one of tranquil happiness. The opening paragraph of this chapter defines such a scene. So does the first sentence of the chapter, when it evokes the "tranquil world" of a "peaceful village" on a Sunday morning. But what follows— Tom's escapades in Sunday school—may seem far from idyllic. Yet, his pranks are essentially harmless and playful, as are all activities that are ordinarily memorialized in idylls.

---

Before Sunday school, Tom focuses his energies on learning by heart five verses from the Bible. In Sunday school, the children earn a small blue ticket for every two verses they recite accurately. Once they have memorized 2000 verses, they can cash in their tickets for 40-cent Bibles. Mary earned two Bibles this way, and a boy "of German parentage" won four or five.

To get Tom to learn his verses, selected from Jesus' Sermon on the Mount (Matthew 5–7), Mary offers him another prize. This turns out to be a

"Barlow" knife—a single-bladed pocket knife of the type first produced in the 1700s by Russell Barlow. Delighted, Tom is about to test its ability to scar the bureau when he has to get washed and dressed.

---

**NOTE: "A man and his brother"**  Twain describes Tom after Mary has washed him as "a man and a brother, without distinction of color." This refers to a medallion that the English ceramics master Josiah Wedgwood designed in 1787. The medallion showed a black man in chains, his hands raised to Heaven, asking, "Am I not a man and a brother?" The motto was quite popular during Twain's youth. It appeared in a variety of places, including at the head of "My Countrymen in Chains," an anti-slavery poem that John Greenleaf Whittier wrote in 1835. What do you think Twain meant to suggest by this reference? Why do you think he compared Tom, when clean, with a slave?

---

At the church, Tom quickly trades the riches he gained in Chapter 2 for the tickets that could earn him a Bible. Inside, the Sunday school superintendent, Mr. Walters, introduces a distinguished visitor, Jeff Thatcher's uncle, Judge Thatcher. The Judge is accompanied by his wife and their child, Becky, whom Tom had tried so hard to impress the day before. Tom begins showing off the moment he sees her. Everyone else, from Mr. Walters to the little girls, tries to win the Judge's attention by showing off, too.

---

**NOTE: Showing off**  Throughout the novel, you'll note adults showing off as much as children. Twain makes fun of his characters' vanity in a gentle, indulgent way. Mr. Walters' fashionable dress is an expression of his vanity just as Aunt Polly's useless glasses are an expression of hers. Everyone in the Sunday school becomes a showoff, aiming their performances at the Thatchers. In what way might the Judge—a distinguished visitor from the town of far-off Constantinople, twelve whole miles away—be putting on a show, too? Where is his audience?

---

As usual, Tom finds a way to steal the spotlight. He steps forward and delivers his tickets to Mr. Walters, who must present him with a Bible. Now Tom is "elevated to a place with the Judge and the other elect."

Tom's heroism is short-lived. When the Judge asks him to name two of Jesus' Twelve Disciples, he can't name one. Instead, he comes up with the names of David, king of the ancient Hebrews, and the giant he slew as a boy.

Twain lets you imagine the way this embarrassing scene ended. What might this chapter have lost if he had provided an ending himself?

## CHAPTER 5

The church service gives the townspeople and their minister, Mr. Sprague, ample chance to show off. It also allows Twain to continue to describe Hannibal's cast of characters and routine happenings.

Twain finds a great deal to mock in the procession of townspeople down the church aisle. The "unnecessary" mayor, the young girls dressed in fancy linen ("lawn-clad"), and their "oiled and simpering admirers." To Tom, the "Model Boy, Willie Mufferson" stands out as particularly noxious. The boys hate Willie, who has been held up by their parents as an example of proper behavior.

---

**NOTE: Twain's asides**   Twain steps into his narrative a couple of times in this chapter to comment on the action. In one instance, he adds an aside about "ill-bred" church choirs. In another, he comments on the "queer custom" of ministers' reeling off announcements. Some readers see these asides as awkward intrusions. Others view them as a fitting part of Twain's unique storytelling style, which he developed while touring as a lecturer. How do the asides affect you?

---

The Reverend Mr. Sprague is an impressive speaker—to his ears and those of other adults, at least. To Tom, he is a bore. During the prayer, Tom focuses on a fly; during the sermon, he counts the pages that Sprague reads from.

---

**NOTE: "Predestined elect"**   To understand one of this chapter's best jokes, you have to know something about the beliefs of the Presbyterian Church. The "predestined elect" are those chosen by God before their deaths to enter Heaven and join God in everlasting joy. Apparently, Sprague has made this designated elite group seem so small that they appear insignificant to Tom, who wonders why such a tiny group should be worth God's notice at all.

---

Tom perks up when the minister describes the millennium—the thousand years of righteousness and happiness that the Bible predicts are coming. According to one prophecy (Isaiah 11:6), animals that were once foes will become friends, with a little child to lead them. This idea appeals to Tom, who would like to be that child—and the center of the world's attention.

Almost accidentally, Tom converts the church service into play, as he does most everything else. Playing with a beetle he has brought to church, he drops it on the aisle, out of his reach. A dog plays with the beetle and gets pinched by it, to the delight of the congregation.

## CHAPTER 6

Twain introduces Huckleberry Finn in this chapter, giving you a chance to compare Tom with a freer spirit. Twain also proceeds with the story of Tom's courtship of Becky.

With a week of school awaiting him when he awakens Monday morning, Tom checks his body for an injury that will allow him to stay home. A "mortified" toe won't do, nor will a loose tooth, which Aunt Polly deftly pulls.

On the way to school, Tom meets Huckleberry Finn, the town drunk's son and the opposite of the model boy. Tom is under orders not to play with Huck. This ban makes Huck more attractive to Tom, who plays with this outcast every chance he gets.

---

**NOTE: The lure of Huck Finn**  In a single paragraph, Twain lists those aspects of Huck Finn's life that make him the envy of "every harassed, hampered, respectable boy in St. Petersburg." The list adds up to total freedom—doing what he pleases, when he pleases, and never having to obey anybody. How are the lives of "respectable boys" like Tom different from Huck's? In what ways are they "hampered?" Might Huck's way of life hamper him in ways that a "respectable" boy like Tom can't imagine?

---

Huck is carrying a dead cat that he bought from another boy. He intends to use the cat at the graveyard that night to cure his warts. He promises to take Tom with him. This promise will allow Twain to introduce one of the novel's major plot lines in Chapter 9.

---

**NOTE: Folklore** The superstitions the boys discuss in this chapter were current in the Midwest during Twain's youth. Thus, they are interesting historically as folklore, which is usually passed on by word of mouth and rarely written down. When it is written down, as here, it enables you to glimpse the way people once thought.

---

Tom's chat with Huck makes him late to school. To everyone's astonishment, he admits he talked to Huck. As punishment, the schoolmaster canes Tom and orders him to sit on the girls' side of the room, in the vacant seat next to Becky Thatcher. This was exactly the "punishment" that Tom had hoped his honesty would bring him.

Once next to Becky, he draws a picture for her,

which she admires. He offers to teach her how to draw during the noon recess, and she agrees. ("Good,—that's a whack," says Tom, meaning "It's a deal.") The teacher catches Tom showing Becky the words "*I love you*," which he has written on the slate. Tom finds himself back in his own seat with a "jubilant" heart. He is unable to focus on his studies—even his best subject, spelling. In a spelling bee, he misses some of the simple words and gets "turned down"—moved from the head of the line to the bottom with each misspelling. In the process, he loses the pewter medal which, as the class's best speller, he had worn for months.

---

**NOTE: Use of the word "nigger"** The first mention of black people in the novel, in Chapter 2, is a reference by the narrator to "negro boys and girls." Here, however, Tom and Huck employ the ugly and disparaging word "nigger." Twain's use of the word has gotten his books labeled racist and banned from some libraries.

Actually, Twain uses the word "nigger" only when trying to give a realistic report of the speech of the people with whom he grew up. When speaking in his own voice—or his narrator's—he usually uses the term "negro," without the capital N that editors of his books often added during this century.

Did he make a mistake by recording the speech current during his boyhood? What might the novel have gained—or lost—if Twain had made Huck and Tom use the word "negro"?

## CHAPTER 7

Twain divides this chapter into two episodes. In the first, you meet Tom's best friend, Joe Harper. The second episode continues the tale of Tom's courtship of Becky Thatcher.

Bored with school, Tom begins to play with the tick that Huck traded him. He devises a game with Joe Harper, who is as intrigued with the bug as Tom is. When the boys argue over the tick, the schoolmaster gets wind of their diversion and whacks them.

During the noon recess, Becky and Tom sneak back into the school. Tom proposes marriage to Becky, who likes the idea of being "engaged" to him. But Tom makes a slip, and Becky realizes that he has been "engaged" before, to Amy Lawrence. Becky refuses to be consoled. Hurt, Tom leaves the school.

## CHAPTER 8

Tom's mood jumps from gloom to delight in this chapter. Note how fantasy and play help him rebound from the sadness caused by a real-world disappointment.

Reacting to Becky's rejection, Tom runs through the woods for a half hour. He finds his way to a familiar spot and thinks how liberating death would be—"if he could only die *temporarily*!" This wish foreshadows the events in Chapter 17, when he attends his own funeral.

He fantasizes becoming a soldier, an Indian chief, and a pirate. What's the point of these fantasies? Are they a kind of revenge—a way of showing "his companions," especially Becky, how dashing a figure they had as a friend? Or is it that projecting himself into romantic situations makes him feel better about himself?

---

**NOTE: Burlesque of Romantic literature**    *The Adventures of Tom Sawyer* is in many ways a burlesque—a takeoff on a literary work or type of work. As already noted, it makes fun of the type of book that shows how good boys (or model boys) prosper. In this chapter's opening paragraph, Tom's brooding appears to many readers as a burlesque of the nineteenth-century convention, in Romantic novels, of the melancholy forest scene. However, Twain uses Tom's imitation of a Romantic hero in another way. Tom's brooding ends with a joke, "if he could only die *temporarily!*" Here, instead of mocking a literary convention, Twain mocks Tom as well. A good part of the novel's humor comes from this gentle indulgence on the part of the narrator.

---

Tom's decision to run away and become a pirate energizes him. He tests a superstition about recovering lost marbles and finds it doesn't work. Yet he refuses to lose faith in superstitions. He convinces himself that a witch made his test fail.

The blast of a toy trumpet announces the start of another episode. Joe Harper appears, pretending to be Guy of Guisborne, and Tom transforms himself into Robin Hood for a series of adventures played "by the book."

---

**NOTE: Tom's literary sources**    Tom, like Sam Clemens as a boy, seems to be an avid reader of swashbuckling romances. Earlier in this chapter, while fancying himself a pirate, he shows his familiarity with Ned Buntline's *The Black Avenger of the Spanish Main, or the Fiend of Blood*, a boys' book published in 1847. The Sherwood Forest adventures that Tom and Joe Harper seem to know by heart come from Joseph Cundall's *Robin Hood and His Merry Foresters*.

## CHAPTER 9

The novel's major plot line—the framing of Muff Potter in Dr. Robinson's murder—begins in this chapter. The chapter also indicates that St. Petersburg has a dark side.

As Tom lies in bed awaiting Huck's appearance, he is frightened by the sound of a beetle (a "deathwatch") ticking in the wall. He believes the superstition that its sound—a watch's ticking—means that someone is about to die. The events that follow won't contradict this belief.

Huck arrives as promised, carrying his dead cat and sounding like a live one. They walk to a graveyard about a mile and a half outside of town.

NOTE: Twain's language   Twain once said, "The difference between the right word and the wrong word is the difference between the lightning and the lightning bug." Watch how carefully Twain chooses his words—especially adjectives and verbs—as he sets his spooky scene here. The fence is "crazy." Grass and weeds grow "rank" (excessive). Old graves are "sunken." "Worm-eaten" boards "staggered" over the graves while a "faint" wind "moaned." Watch for other examples of Twain's suggestive imagery.

The "solemnity and silence" of the graveyard keep the boys quiet while they hide a few feet from Hoss Williams' fresh grave. The sound of people approaching terrifies them. For a moment Huck thinks a lantern is "devil-fire"—the burning of gases released by decaying matter. Soon they realize that they are in the presence not of devils but of three men they know: Muff Potter, a good-for-nothing; Injun Joe, a "half-breed"; and Dr. Robinson, a young physician from the town. Dr. Robinson has hired the others to dig up Hoss Williams' body so that he can experiment on it. (Because of legal restrictions, there was always a shortage of cadavers for doctors and medical students to study, and the practice of grave robbing, or body snatching, was not uncommon.)

When Hoss Williams' body has been dug up and tied to a wheelbarrow, Potter and Injun Joe demand more money. The men fight. Robinson knocks out Potter, and Injun Joe murders Robinson with Potter's knife. Tom and Huck, caught up in a real adventure and not a fantasy, leap up and flee.

The narrator lingers behind to report the murder's aftermath. Injun Joe robs Robinson's body and places the murder weapon in Potter's hand. When Potter comes to, Joe convinces him that he (Potter) murdered the doctor; Potter trots off, leaving his knife behind.

**NOTE: Injun Joe's vengefulness**  Twain goes to some length to provide Injun Joe with a motive for

killing Robinson. Injun Joe feels he was mistreated
five years earlier when the Robinsons refused him
food and had him jailed as a vagrant. Injun Joe's
vengefulness is a key to his character—one that
will explain his later actions and terrify Tom and
Huck into silence.

# CHAPTER 10

This chapter serves as an interlude, allowing Tom
and Huck to catch their breath—literally and fig-
uratively. It also serves as a transition back to the
civilized world of aunts, school, and young love.

The boys flee to an old tannery (where leather
is made) on the outskirts of St. Petersburg. They
mull over the murder and what they ought to do
about it. They decide it's safest to keep quiet. "That
Injun devil wouldn't make any more of drownding
us than a couple of cats," Huck says. With their
blood, they initial a pledge of silence that Tom writes
on a pine shingle with red chalk. Huck, who doesn't
understand how painful writing is for Tom, admires Tom's choice of words and the ease with
which he seems (to Huck, at least) to write them.

The boys' superstitions cause them some fright
when a dog howls outside the tannery. They believe that the howling of a stray dog spells death
for anyone the dog is facing. The howling stops
and is replaced with loud snoring. Relieved and
feeling adventurous once more, they tiptoe to the
snorer, who turns out to be Muff Potter. As they
escape, they see the howling dog facing Potter and
believe he's the one who's doomed.

Tom doesn't know that Sid is awake when he
sneaks into their bedroom. In the morning, Polly

lets him oversleep. After breakfast, she takes him aside and cries over his behavior. Her tears, to Tom, are "worse than a thousand whippings."

He mopes off to school, where the schoolmaster flogs him for playing hooky the previous afternoon. The final blow to his self-esteem comes when he sits down at his desk and finds that Becky Thatcher has returned the brass andiron knob he had given her.

---

**NOTE: Contrasts between Tom and Huck**  This chapter gives you a chance to explore further the differences between Huck and Tom. Clearly, Tom is the more educated of the two. He thinks up the oath, writes it, and teaches Huck to scrawl his initials. But Huck has "street smarts." He knows how important it is for his and Tom's safety to keep his mouth shut. He also knows that ensuring silence requires a pledge as solemn as a blood oath. Tom's suggestion—"you just hold hands and swear"— is, as Huck points out, inappropriate for "a big thing like this." At this point in the story, Huck seems the more practical and down-to-earth of the two. As you read on, watch to see if he stays that way.

---

## CHAPTER 11

This chapter adds weight to the opinion that St. Petersburg is not an entirely idyllic place. Mixed with the nostalgia are corpses, citizens ready to condemn the innocent before trial, and haunting nightmares.

The discovery of Dr. Robinson's body electrifies

the town. The schoolmaster gives the students the afternoon off, and the townspeople flock to the graveyard.

The murder weapon has been found and identified as Muff Potter's. So, when he turns up—seeking his knife—the sheriff confronts him with the evidence. Broken, he tells Injun Joe, who is in the crowd, to explain what happened. Huck and Tom stand dumbfounded as they listen to the real murderer pin the crime on Potter.

When Injun Joe helps put Robinson's corpse in a wagon, the body seems to bleed a little. According to superstition—a corpse bleeds when its murderer is near. But since Muff Potter is only three feet away at the time, no one in the superstitious crowd except Huck and Tom thinks to suspect Injun Joe.

Tom has begun crying out in his sleep, so tormented is he by his secret knowledge. Sid is eager to crack the mystery, and Tom is just as eager to hide it. Tom pretends he has a toothache so that he can tie his jaw closed at night to keep himself from talking.

In time, Tom is haunted less and less by nightmares. To ease his conscience, he smuggles "small comforts" to Potter, who has been jailed in "a little brick den" on the side of the village.

The boys aren't the only people in town who are afraid of Injun Joe. Some want to tar-and-feather him for his part in the body-snatching, but no one has the courage to do it.

---

**NOTE: Parallels with Twain's childhood**   When Twain was eighteen, in 1853, he gave some matches to a drunken tramp who had been put in Hannibal's jail—an unguarded place very much like the one Potter is held in here. That night the tramp accidentally set fire to his cell and burned to death. Twain recalled years later that the tramp "lay upon my conscience a hundred nights afterwards and filled them with hideous dreams." How might his feelings about the tramp have helped Twain understand Tom's guilt over Potter?

# CHAPTER 12

Twain offers you some comic relief in this chapter. The episode serves as a bridge between two story lines: the murder and its aftermath, and Tom's running away to Jackson's Island in Chapter 13.

The chapter uses another plot line—Tom's courtship of Becky Thatcher—as a springboard. Becky is sick, and her absence from school takes all the joy out of Tom's life. It seems that Becky's sickness is one thing that Tom can't transform into play.

Yet Aunt Polly manages to turn Tom's woe into a form of play for herself. She loves to experiment with patent (non-prescription) medicines, and Tom's depression provides a challenge to her inventiveness.

NOTE: **Model for Polly's quackery**  As early as 1866, when Twain was on a steamer headed for Hawaii, he jotted down memories that would become part of *Tom Sawyer*. Some of those notes described his mother's attempts to make him swallow a patent medicine called Pain-Killer (spelled, incorrectly, Painkiller in some editions). The med-

icine was supposed to be used externally to soothe
aching muscles and bruises. But his mother, an
avid reader of the "quack periodicals" Twain crit-
icizes here, thought that Pain-Killer might have in-
ternal uses, as well. Twain, in turn, gave a dose
of the medicine to his cat—with the consequences
he elaborates on in this chapter.

Tom can't hide from Polly's "persecution." But,
despite his gloominess, he finds a defense, once
more, in a game from which he will emerge vic-
torious. He pretends to want her Pain-Killer so much
that she finally allows him to serve himself, and
Tom pours doses of the vile liquid through a crack
in the floor. While he is doing this, Peter, the cat,
begs for a taste. Tom gives him one, and Peter
leaps around the room in pain. "Cats always act
so when they're having a good time," he tells Polly.

He continues speaking ironically—saying one
thing and meaning another—even after Polly discovers what has happened. "I done it out of pity
for him—because he hadn't any aunt." Tom now
has Polly where he wants her—feeling remorseful.
"What was cruelty to a cat *might* be cruelty to a
boy, too," she allows. Tom has won his game.

But the chapter ends in defeat for him. He sets
off to school early and hangs around the schoolyard gate hoping to see Becky Thatcher. She shows
up, and Tom is suddenly beside himself with happiness. But his showing off only brings a reproach
from Becky, crushing him.

**NOTE: Tom's behavior**  Some readers aren't
amused by Tom's strenuous efforts to gain atten-

tion. "Adults might think such antics are cute,"
Robert Keith Miller writes in his book, *Mark Twain*.
"But they're not the ones being knocked over or
having their hat snatched. The actual victims of
his aggression probably welcomed the days on
which Tom chose to stay away from school." What
do you think Tom's classmates feel about him?
Could Twain's nostalgia for his boyhood lead him
to overlook the fact that Tom might be a nuisance?
Or are such speculations beside the point?

# CHAPTER 13

A third story line—Tom's running away with Joe
Harper and Huck—begins with this chapter. This
story will be the focus of the novel for five chapters.

Driven away by the two girls he loves—Polly
and Becky—Tom sulks. He convinces himself that
he has been forced to "lead a life of crime." The
school bell rings as he walks away from it, and he
sobs. Tom meets Joe Harper, who also plans to
run away. Tom persuades him to become a pirate.
Once more, Tom's fantasies, gleaned from books,
overpower a comrade.

NOTE: "Two souls," etc. Twain calls Joe and Tom
"two souls with but a single thought." This is a
reference to the last two lines of *Ingomar the Bar-
barian*, a play by Von Munch Bellinghausen that
Twain saw in Virginia City, Nevada, in 1863. The
play ends, "Two souls with but a single thought,
two hearts that beat as one." Evidently, Twain believed that his readers would recognize the quote.

The boys decide to run away to Jackson's Island—Twain's fictional name for Glasscock's Island, opposite Hannibal. They get Huckleberry Finn to join them. The three boys steal provisions and meet at midnight two miles above the village.

They are clearly enacting an adventure—one right out of storybooks that Tom has read. Note the gallant names: Tom, "the Black Avenger"; Huck Finn "the Red-Handed"; and Joe "the Terror of the Seas." Ned Buntline's *Black Avenger*, noted earlier, is the source of Tom's nickname. Buntline's 1847 book, *The Last Days of Callao*, may be the source of Huck's nickname. In that book, a pirate ship hoists a white flag emblazoned with "a blood-red hand."

They steal a raft and head out into the Mississippi. Tom, naturally, is in charge—after all, it's *his* fantasy. His companions man the oars.

---

**NOTE: Twain's style**   Twain's use of words, especially in descriptive passages about nature, can be quite beautiful. Take a moment to savor his description of the boys' nighttime view of St. Petersburg, "peacefully sleeping, beyond the vague vast sweep of star-gemmed water. . . ." You might want to note poetic passages like this and write about them later in a consideration of Twain's style.

---

The raft drifts downstream five miles and comes to rest on the north end of Jackson's Island, where they make camp.

Afterwards, they have a discussion that accentuates the differences between Huck and the other two boys. Tom and Joe are thrilled to think that their classmates would envy them. Huck doesn't care what others think. Nor is he happy, as Tom is, not to have to "go to school, and wash"—things Huck never does anyway. Huck is content to be eating well and to be out of range of St. Petersburg's respectable citizens, who badger ("bullyrag") him.

Huck lights a pipe and smokes it—something the other boys have never done. He's ashamed of his clothes. "I ain't dressed fitten for a pirate," he concludes. Yet he sleeps easily. The other boys, more accustomed to telling right from wrong, feel guilty and have trouble falling asleep.

# CHAPTER 14

This chapter describes the boys' first full day on Jackson's Island. It is a day of roller-coaster mood swings, especially for Joe and Tom. Notice how plot twists shape the boys' moods and how the moods, in turn, shape the story.

The chapter opens with a long description of the island's animal life "shaking off sleep and going to work." The boys spend most of the day swimming, fishing, and exploring the island. Late in the afternoon, they begin to feel homesick.

The booming of cannon on the ferryboat interrupts their thoughts. They realize that the boat is trying to locate the body of someone who has drowned. (During Twain's youth people believed that the concussion of the cannon blasts were capable of bursting a sunken corpse's gall bladder, causing it to float to the surface.) It's Tom who understands who is thought to have "drownded—it's us!" Nothing more wonderful had ever happened to them. They are the talk of St. Petersburg.

After dinner, however, their thoughts become

more somber. Tom and Joe begin to feel guilty about the grief they've caused their families. But when Joe suggests they return home, Tom makes him feel foolish. Tom stays awake after the others fall asleep. He writes two notes on sycamore bark, pockets one, and places the other in Joe's hat. Then he bolts toward the sandbar. What's on his mind?

# CHAPTER 15

This chapter explains Tom's secrecy and sets the stage for the next two chapters. It also gives you a glimpse of Tom as a genuinely loving nephew.

Tom wades, then swims to the Illinois shore, where he hides in a rowboat tied to the stern of the ferry and is towed back to Missouri. In St. Petersburg, he sneaks into Polly's house and crawls under her bed in the sitting room. Sid, Polly, Mary, and Joe Harper's mother are at the table, bemoaning the lost children. Their words give Tom a "nobler opinion of himself than ever before."

Tom's earlier hope of dying—temporarily—has come true. He hears his former tormentors grieve over him and he's overwhelmed, partly with pride, partly with love for his aunt. He learns that the boys' funerals will be held Sunday morning—four days away.

After Mrs. Harper leaves, Polly goes to bed. Her prayer for Tom is so moving, it makes him cry. She falls asleep, and Tom creeps over to the table, where the candle still burns, and leaves the note he wrote for her. But a thought makes him change his mind. He pockets the note, kisses his sleeping aunt, and exits. He rows back to the Illinois shore and, after sunrise, swims back to Jackson's Island. After recounting his adventures, he sleeps until noon while Huck and Joe play.

**NOTE: Tom's craftiness**    Skillful storytellers build suspense by withholding enough of their stories to keep readers turning pages. Twain does this here, raising questions about Tom's goals, revealing them by describing his journey home, then creating another mystery by having Tom pocket the note he has written to Polly. Interestingly, Twain's narrative method parallels Tom's method as a strategist. Tom keeps his goals a secret from his family and friends until he can reveal them with a final dramatic flourish. In Chapter 12, he plotted a game designed to stop Polly from persecuting him with Pain-Killer, and he never revealed his goal until he had Polly cornered. Similarly, he doesn't let his friends know the purpose of his trip home. Can you guess why he is so slow to show his hand?

# CHAPTER 16

In terms of writing and character development, this is one of the richest chapters in the novel. It's all the more remarkable because it seems no more than a description of two days of play for the three "pirates." Examine it closely, however, and you'll see how skillful Twain is at depicting the anguish of three boys trying ever so hard to become men.

After breakfast Friday morning, they shed their clothes and frolic in the water. Later, they play marbles: "knucks" (shooters must keep their knuckles on the ground), "ring-taw" (shooters knock marbles out of the ring), and "keeps" (players keep the marbles they win). Tom, his superstitions intact, refuses to follow the others into the water for a second swim because he has lost his lucky charm—an anklet made of rattlesnake rattles, which he believes can ward off a variety of sicknesses.

The three boys all struggle to subdue feelings of homesickness. Tom tries to divert his friends' attention from their misery but fails. Joe finally admits he wants to go home. Tom is determined not to let him.

---

**NOTE: Joe's confession** Joe's admission that he wants to go home sets him apart from Huck and Tom. Tom calls him a crybaby and mocks him for wanting to see his mother. This attempt to embarrass Joe into staying reminds you that Joe is the only one of the three who has a mother to return to.

---

As Joe begins to wade toward the Illinois shore, Huck says he wants to leave, too. Tom is able to stop them only by playing his trump card. He reveals "his secret"—which Twain refuses, at this point, to reveal to you. Tom's craftiness surfaces here. He had planned all along to reveal his scheme, but only as a "last seduction" to keep the boys on the island. The ploy works.

After lunch, Huck teaches his friends how to smoke. Tom and Joe pretend to like smoking. But the dominant feeling is nausea. Joe excuses himself by saying he must hunt for his knife, and Tom offers to help. An hour later, Huck looks for them and finds them asleep. There are indications that both have been sick.

That night, Joe wakes his friends as a storm brews. The boys sit by the fire, waiting for something to happen. Beyond the fire, "everything was swallowed up in the blackness of darkness"—one of Twain's favorite biblical phrases. It comes from the New Testament Book of Jude, where false teachers are compared with shooting stars that flare up only to be lost forever "in the blackness of darkness."

Saturday morning, they sleep a little in the sun and are soon overcome with homesickness. Tom manages to lift their spirits by organizing a game of Indians, and they pass the day chasing each other around the island. For Tom and Joe, the day is almost ruined at the end, when, according to customs they've read or heard about, they must puff a peace pipe. To their delight, they discover that this time they don't get "sick enough to be seriously uncomfortable."

After supper, they smoke again. This new skill makes them happier than "the scalping and skinning of the Six Nations." This is a reference to the powerful Iroquois confederation—originally of five tribes (the Mohawks, Oneidas, Onondagas, Senecas, and Cayugas), later of six, after the Tuscaroras joined them around 1722. These tribes dominated the western part of what is today New York State.

---

NOTE: Understanding Twain's allusions   Why is it worth your while to track down these allusions, or passing references, such as the mention of the Six Nations and the phrase from the Book of Jude? For one thing, the effort gives you a deeper appreciation of The Adventures of Tom Sawyer as literature and as a historical document. It leads you to a deeper understanding of the text—of Twain's

meaning and the way he expresses it. In addition,
the references are clues to the way Twain's con-
temporaries thought, and to what they thought
about. For example, Indians were much on Americans' minds in the 1870s. (General George Custer
made his famous "last stand" against the Sioux in
1876, the year *Tom Sawyer* was published.) Also, it
was a rare American family that didn't own a Bible
and refer to it regularly. Biblical stories and teach-
ings shaped the way Americans thought, and biblical phrases cropped up in conversation the way
lines from popular songs do now.

## CHAPTER 17

Twain reveals Tom's secret in this short chapter,
which provides the climax of the Jackson's Island
adventure. As you read, note how subtly Twain
uses irony to bring out the underlying humor of
this elaborate practical joke.

On Saturday, while the boys are playing Indians
on Jackson's Island, the town of St. Petersburg is
shrouded with grief. Becky, in tears, wishes she
had kept the brass andiron knob "to remember
[Tom] by." Elsewhere, children envy those among
them who were the last to see the boys alive.

On Sunday, the boys' funerals take the place of
the regular church service. The minister's "text"—
the New Testament passage that introduces the
subject of his sermon—is John 11:25–26. In this
passage, common at funerals, Jesus promises life
after death to people who believe Him to be the
"resurrection and the life"—the giver of eternal
life. Would the boys qualify as believers? For evi-

dence, you might reread Tom and Huck's exchange inside the tannery in Chapter 10.

---

**NOTE: Use of irony**  Twain shows himself a master of irony—saying one thing while suggesting another—in this chapter. Note especially how he describes the minister's "pictures of the graces, the winning ways and the rare promise of the lost lads." Of course, few people—probably including the minister—ever saw anything but "faults and flaws" in the boys. The funeral sermon is a literary convention (a generally accepted form) that regularly transforms sinners into saints, and Twain gently mocks that convention here.

Note that though he may be stretching the truth, the minister is not speaking ironically. He wants his listeners to believe he is sincere. It's Twain who is being ironic. He presents alternative interpretations of the boys' characters and pranks to suggest that the minister's view of the boys' "sweet, generous natures" may be inaccurate. Inaccurate, perhaps, but convincing. At the end, even the minister is in tears!

---

As if on cue, a miracle occurs. The boys are resurrected, just as the Bible passage promised they would be. Tom, Joe, and Huck march up the aisle after having heard their funeral sermon from the empty gallery above the congregation. Twain reveals Tom's secret scheme at last.

Dumbfounded, the minister orders the congregation to sing the Doxology—a hymn of praise for God. ("Old Hundred," the tune to which the Doxology is sung, is so called because Psalm 100 was once sung to it.) Tom swells with pride, confessing to himself "that this was the proudest moment of his life."

Remarkably, no one is angry with the boys. The townspeople have had such a good time that they feel it was worth being "sold" (tricked) and made to look ridiculous.

---

**NOTE: The funeral as entertainment** Tom, as you've seen, transforms everything he can into play, with himself as the central figure. Here, he turns his funeral into entertainment—not just for himself, but for the entire town. Like Huck and Joe on Jackson's Island, or the boys who paint Polly's fence, the townspeople become willing participants in the fun and end up grateful to Tom for orchestrating it.

---

## CHAPTER 18

With this chapter, Twain begins to discard the plot line that described the escapade on Jackson's Island. He returns Tom to "the world of the living"—and to Tom's difficult courtship of Becky Thatcher.

Twain opens with a paragraph that ties up loose ends about the boys' return to St. Petersburg. Then he moves on to breakfast before school Monday morning. Polly can't understand how Tom let her believe he was dead.

To make her feel better, he says, "I dreamed about you, anyway. That's something, ain't it?" At Polly's urging, he tells her about his "dream," a detailed description of the activities he witnessed from beneath Polly's bed. Polly is amazed at this clairvoyance—the ability to see things that one does not witness in person—and rewards him with an apple.

At school, Tom and Joe are heroes. They embellish their adventures with imaginary "material" and dazzle their friends with their new skill—smoking.

Tom decides to play hard-to-get with Becky. While she tries to gain his attention, he carries on an animated conversation with Amy Lawrence. Becky vows to get even. At recess, she sits with Alfred Temple, the new boy from St. Louis with whom Tom fought in Chapter 1. Tom, incensed, suddenly finds Amy's chirping "intolerable."

Tom goes home at noon, beside himself with jealousy. Once Tom is gone, Becky loses interest in Alfred Temple and dismisses him. Smart enough to realize why, he slips into the deserted schoolhouse and spills ink on Tom's spelling book. Although Becky sees Alfred do this, she is so angry with Tom that she decides to let him be punished for something he didn't do.

---

**NOTE: Becky's character** This chapter gives you a deeper understanding of Becky. Like Tom, she is an interesting figure because she is not a model child. Although she is certainly better behaved than Tom, she has certain traits—a quick temper, a vindictive spirit, and a tendency to show off—that would have made her unacceptable as a heroine in most children's books of Twain's day.

# CHAPTER 19

With this brief chapter, Twain gives Tom a chance to redeem himself with Polly—and with you, if you have begun to wonder, like Polly, whether Tom's heart is made of stone.

Tom returns home from school to discover that Aunt Polly is furious with him. That morning she went to Sereny Harper's house to tell her about Tom's "dream." But Mrs. Harper had a surprise for *her*. She told Polly that Tom had secretly visited St. Petersburg. Polly wonders how Tom could have let her make a fool of herself in front of Mrs. Harper.

Tom is genuinely remorseful. His joke, the narrator tells you, now seems "mean and shabby" to him. He apologizes lamely to Polly, explaining that he "didn't think." Still, Polly doesn't believe him when he says he returned home to tell her "not to be uneasy about us." Tom explains that he pocketed the sycamore bark note because he couldn't "bear to spoil" the idea of attending his own funeral.

Polly's soft side begins to show. When Tom tells her he kissed her as she slept, "a sudden tenderness dawned in her eyes." Tom says he kissed her because he loves her. Does this sound like Tom to you? To Polly, it sounds like he's telling the truth—but she's not sure. She sends Tom off to school and immediately runs to the closet to dig into his jacket pocket for the sycamore bark note.

At this point, a wonderful piece of stage business illustrates Twain's weakness for sight gags. Polly tries to get up the nerve to check Tom's pockets, but she is afraid she'll discover that Tom is lying to her. She holds his jacket—then puts it back.

Twice she reaches into the closet, and twice her hand comes out without the jacket. The third time, she convinces herself that, if he is lying, "it's a good lie—I won't let it grieve me."

To her surprise, the note Tom wrote her *is* there. She reads it through "flowing tears" and admits she could forgive him now "if he'd committed a million sins."

## CHAPTER 20

Twain continues to "rehabilitate" Tom in the eyes of those readers who might think Tom went too far in some of his earlier pranks. For the first time, you see Tom make a real sacrifice and not just dream about doing so.

As the noon break ends, Polly has sent Tom back to school in high spirits. His good mood prompts him to apologize to Becky for being mean to her that morning. But Becky is unforgiving. In the schoolyard, the two exchange insults, and Becky can't wait to see Tom flogged for the ink Alfred Temple spilled on his book.

Soon Becky is in a fix herself. Before school resumes, she sneaks a look at the schoolmaster's anatomy book, which he keeps under lock and key. Tom surprises her, and she accidentally rips the page on which a naked figure was printed.

---

**NOTE: Hint of sex**   As previously noted, Tom is a curiously ageless boy, seeming anywhere from eight to fourteen. You may think this is a flaw in Tom's characterization, as many readers do. But others point out that by making Tom's age indeterminate, Twain freed himself to write about *boyhood* instead of a single boy.

This broader approach may explain why the subject of sex is so blurry in Tom's world. In Chapter 7, Tom explains kissing to Becky, who acts as if she's never heard of the practice before. Here, Twain fails to tell you whether the "stark naked" figure in the anatomy book is male or female.

As Twain first wrote it, this scene did have the children confront the mystery of sex. Twain emphasized the nature of the picture as much as the rip in the page. "How could I know it wasn't a nice book?" Tom originally said. "I didn't know girls ever—." And Becky, after worrying about being whipped for tearing the page, told Tom: "But that isn't anything—it ain't *half*. You'll tell everybody about the picture, and O, O, O!" In revision, Twain deleted these words and a passage in which Tom realizes how the revelation might shame Becky.

From what you know about late nineteenth-century attitudes about morality, why do you think Twain made these changes?

---

Becky tells Tom how terrified she is of a whipping. "I never was whipped in school," she says. This assertion indicates that she fears the pain less than the indignity of the punishment. Becky assumes that Tom is going to tell on her. She tells him ominously, "*I* know something that's going to happen. You just wait and you'll see!"

Sure enough, Tom gets whipped for the mess Alfred Temple made of his spelling book. Becky refuses to intervene because she's sure Tom will tell Dobbins what she did to the anatomy text.

An hour later, Dobbins discovers the tear in his book. He begins to ask individual students if they're to blame. Becky is "white with terror" and seems about to give herself away when Tom springs to his feet and shouts, "*I* done it!" Though Tom had no selfish motive—he wanted only to protect Becky—he is well rewarded for his bravery. He takes his flogging in front of Becky's adoring eyes.

Tom goes to bed that night plotting vengeance on Alfred Temple, whose deed Becky has told him about. As he drops off to sleep, he remembers Becky's words: "Tom, how *could* you be so noble!"

---

NOTE: **Becky's vengefulness**  Becky's less-than-model character was noted in the discussion of Chapter 18. In Chapter 20, she lets Tom take the blame for something she knows he didn't do. Twain provides her with a motive—she fears Tom will tell on her and wants to see him hurt, too. But the contrast between her behavior and Tom's selfless action raises several questions. Does Becky's motive excuse her behavior? Why doesn't Tom seem angry about the deceit? Finally, what do you make of the fact that for once Tom has become a model boy? Is he maturing?

---

# CHAPTER 21

Faced with patent insincerity, the indulgent narrator takes off his gloves here. Twain has tucked an expository essay into this chapter to explain his anger and some of his views on writing. Yet the chapter is still hilariously funny.

As the school year winds down, Mr. Dobbins prepares his students for the ordeal of Examination Night, the closing exercise. Dobbins is especially eager for a good performance. He literally whips his students into shape—at least, those students too small to fight back. Remember that the one-room schoolhouse of Twain's day served students of all ages. The oldest student in Twain's school, Andy Fuqua, was twenty-five.

The smaller boys hatch a plot to get revenge on Examination Night. Except to say that the sign-painter's boy has been enlisted in the scheme, Twain keeps you in the dark about the plot until the very end of the chapter. Can you suggest why?

The bulk of the chapter describes Examination Night. Read the description closely to discover Twain's criticism of a popular literary style and of what passed for education in his day.

The entire town seems to have assembled to see the students perform and compete for prizes. The first "scholar" to appear is a little boy, who recites an old favorite—David Everett's 1791 poem, "Lines Written for a School Declamation by a Little Boy of Seven." (Twain provides only the first two lines.) Although his delivery is unnatural (his gestures are like those of a machine "a trifle out of order") and he is "cruelly scared," the boy survives the experience.

Tom Sawyer does not survive his. He struggles through Patrick Henry's 1775 speech to the Virginia Convention, is seized with stage fright, and leaves the stage "utterly defeated."

---

**NOTE: Tom's failure**   Tom loves the limelight and will do almost anything to be the center of attention. But those occasions when he is the focus of attention in academic settings are excruciatingly painful. In Chapter 4, when pressed to name Jesus' first two disciples, he is so far off base that

Twain draws "the curtain of charity over the rest of the scene." How do you explain Tom's success at schemes that he designs and controls and his failure at those designed by others?

Following Tom's defeat, others recite such "declamatory gems" as Felicia D. Hemans' "Casabianca" and Lord Byron's "The Destruction of Sennacherib." (Twain refers to these poems respectively by their first lines, "The boy stood on the burning deck" and "The Assyrian came down.") The night includes a spelling bee, recitations in Latin, and reading exercises.

But the evening's highlight comes when the older girls read their original essays, which Twain reviews with disdain. As Twain notes at the end of the chapter, he did not create these examples of "schoolgirl prose." He lifted them, word-for-word, from Mary Ann Harris Gay's 1871 book, *The Pastor's Story and Other Pieces: or, Prose and Poetry*.

**NOTE: Twain's criticisms** What irks Twain about these "original 'compositions?' " First, they're not very original. "The themes were the same that had been illuminated upon similar occasions by . . . all their ancestors in the female line clear back to the Crusades." Second, the compositions are full of overworked melancholy. Third, they are wordy and artificially pumped up with "fine language." Fourth, their authors re-use pet words and phrases until they are "worn entirely out." Fifth, they are "marred" by preachiness—"the intolerable sermon that wagged its crippled tail at the end of each and every one of them." In sum, the essays are unfelt and insincere.

By implication, Twain's criticism condemns the adult world that encourages insincerity. The adult listeners whisper such compliments as "How eloquent!" and "So true!" during the readings and applaud enthusiastically.

Is Twain being too harsh on the authors and their parents? You can't answer accurately until you've applied Twain's standards to the three excerpts he includes in this chapter. You might also ask yourself how Twain might grade some of the essays you or your classmates have written. How free is Twain's own writing of the flaws he describes?

The chapter ends with a bigger joke—the scheme of revenge that the smaller boys have devised. Dobbins is trying to draw a map of the U.S. on the blackboard when a hatch door leading to the attic opens above him. The boys lower a blindfolded cat on a string. The cat snatches Dobbins' wig, baring his bald, gold-painted head—the work of the sign-painter's boy, at whose house Dobbins lives.

**NOTE: Twain's comic method**   Take a moment to analyze this joke. Suppose Dobbins' head hadn't been painted and the boys had pulled off the wig with a fishhook instead of a cat. The gag would still be funny. But the extra elements—the cat, the cat's blindfold, and the gold paint—make the joke hilarious. What does the elaborateness of the joke add to it?

___

# CHAPTER 22

This chapter, along with the last one, acts as a bridge between plot lines. Two chapters back, Twain took a break from the story of Tom's courtship of Becky. Now Tom marks time during the first weeks of summer until Twain, in Chapter 23, picks up the threads of the murder story with Muff Potter's trial. Twain, however, doesn't waste your time here. He presents an entertaining review of small-town life before movies, TV, and radio provided the distractions they do today.

Tom is attracted to the temperance movement not by any urge to stamp out drinking and smoking but by the chance to wear a showy uniform. Just as Huck Finn became an irresistible companion when parents forbade their children to play with him, Tom is now tormented by an urge to drink and swear—two things he promised not to do when he joined the Cadets of Temperance.

___

NOTE: Cadets of Temperance　This organizational actually existed in the late 1840s and early 1850s. It was part of the youth wing of the national temperance movement that campaigned vigorously against alcohol and smoking. Twain joined the cadets when he was about fifteen. He pledged not to smoke in exchange for the privilege of wearing a red merino (wool and cotton) sash during public holidays and parades. "The organization was weak and impermanent," Twain concluded in his

*Autobiography*, "because there were not enough holidays to support it." He remained a cadet "until I had gathered the glory of two displays—May Day and the Fourth of July." Then he resigned and resumed smoking—something he had been doing since he was nine.

---

Tom stays in the organization because a prominent public figure, Judge Frazer, is on his deathbed, and Tom foresees a chance to march in his funeral. But the judge takes a turn for the better. Tom, in disgust, resigns from the lodge, and that very night the judge dies. Now Tom must watch the funeral parade with envy. No longer bound by his pledge, he loses the urge to drink and swear.

Looking for amusement, he begins a diary but can't think of anything to write in it. A minstrel show—a variety show of music, dancing, and comedy performed by white people made up as blacks—comes to town and is a sensation. Led by Tom and Joe Harper, the children devise their own minstrel act and are "happy for two days."

---

NOTE: Minstrel shows  Before movies and TV, small towns like St. Petersburg had to import their entertainment or manufacture their own. Lecturers—Twain himself would become one of the best— were popular. So were circuses and troupes of actors who crisscrossed the nation performing one or two plays. Minstrel shows first appeared in 1843 in Virginia and were nationally popularized by such troupes as Edwin P. Christy's, which was founded in Buffalo, New York, in 1846. In their use of dialect, dance movements, and humor, the minstrel shows caricatured black people and, in so doing, planted damaging stereotypes in white people's minds.

The summer plods on, with each high point followed by a low one. Missouri's most famous politician, U.S. Senator Thomas Hart Benton (1782–1858), proves a disappointment to Tom when he makes an appearance at the July 4th parade. A phrenologist and a mesmerizer (hypnotist) break the monotony. (Phrenologists claimed to be able to "read" peoples' character traits by feeling the contours of their scalps.) Becky's absence (she has returned to her parents' home in Constantinople for vacation), the "dreadful secret of murder," and finally the measles keep Tom at a low ebb.

After he recovers from the measles, Tom discovers that an evangelist has passed through town and that everybody has "got religion." Even Huck is quoting the Bible. Tom concludes that as the only irreligious person in town he is doomed to eternal damnation. A driving rainstorm confirms his fears. He is sure that God is trying to punish him for his sins, and he is grateful to find himself alive when the storm ends. Yet he doesn't change his ways and become more religious. In Tom's view, that proves to be a mistake, because he suffers a relapse and has to spend the next three weeks in bed.

NOTE: Tom's "Presbyterian conscience"  Twain often spoke of his "Presbyterian conscience"—a sense of guilt stemming from the belief that, one way or another, all sins had to be answered for.

The corollary held that any setback—sickness, bankruptcy, storm damage, even violent death— was a punishment for sin. As a boy, Twain, like Tom, was haunted by guilt. "Mine was a trained Presbyterian conscience," he wrote in his *Autobiography*, "and [it] knew but the one duty—to hunt and harry its slave upon all pretexts and on all occasions, particularly when there was no sense nor reason in it." How might this "Presbyterian conscience" explain some of Tom's fears and nightmares and the "chronic misery" of keeping his secret about the murder?

# CHAPTER 23

The plot line that concerns Dr. Robinson's murder ends with Muff Potter's trial and Tom's testimony, which provides the climax of the story (and, some readers feel, of the novel itself). As the murder story is resolved, a fourth story begins, involving the fate of Injun Joe.

Muff Potter's trial for murder brings the sleepy town to life. Tom and Huck wrestle with their consciences. But they won't come forth and tell what they know about the murder for fear Injun Joe will kill them.

During the first two days of the trial, the boys hang around outside the courthouse and learn that things are going poorly for Potter. Tom stays out late the night of the second day, although Twain doesn't explain why. Tom's "tremendous state of excitement" keeps him awake for several hours. Can you imagine where he has been?

The courthouse is packed on the third day of the trial. Tom takes the stand as a surprise witness.

He glances at Injun Joe and is at first speechless. Yet he finds his voice and explains that he and someone else (Potter's lawyer counsels him not to reveal Huck's name yet) saw Muff Potter knocked out and Dr. Robinson murdered by Injun Joe.

At these words, Injun Joe leaps through the window and disappears. Thus ends the story of Dr. Robinson's murder. But its resolution creates another mystery and a fourth plot line. What will happen to Injun Joe? Will he try to kill Tom and Huck, as the boys feared?

---

**NOTE: Tom's maturation**   Does Tom's bravery surprise you? It shouldn't, because Twain has carefully prepared you for it with a parallel episode, where Tom took the blame for Becky after she tore Mr. Dobbins' anatomy book. He seems to have reached a stage in his moral development where he is not merely able to tell the difference between right and wrong but also to act what he believes is right.

How does he differ from Huck in this regard? Why didn't Huck step forward with Tom, or instead of Tom? Some readers feel that, as a child of the streets, Huck lives by a code that puts his own survival first. Others explain the difference between the two boys by pointing to Tom's "Presbyterian conscience"—his fear of God's wrath. Watch for further evidence of Tom's maturity in the remaining chapters.

---

## CHAPTER 24

The next ten chapters largely concern Injun Joe's fate. This chapter describes the aftermath of Tom's testimony and builds suspense by reminding you several times that the murderer is still at large.

Tom is a genuine hero. His celebrity, though delicious to him, does little to calm his fears. His nights are "seasons of horror," terrorized by dreams of Injun Joe.

Huck is terrified that Injun Joe might hear that he witnessed the murder, too. Potter's lawyer has promised to tell no one. But Huck has lost faith in such promises, now that Tom has broken the blood oath between them.

Tom fears that he will never be safe until he has seen Injun Joe's corpse. Remember this statement. It foreshadows the resolution of this plot line by setting—in Tom's eyes—the only acceptable terms for a successful outcome.

A big-city detective from St. Louis arrives to investigate the case. He finds a clue (Twain spelled it "clew")—hardly a substitute for Injun Joe's corpse.

---

**NOTE: Outsiders**  The citizens of St. Petersburg are in awe of outsiders such as the detective from St. Louis and Judge Thatcher, whose "very eyes had looked upon the county court house," twelve miles away in Constantinople. By citing the townspeople's exalted view of outsiders, Twain demonstrates that St. Petersburg is small and isolated enough to give its residents an inferiority complex. However, the narrator's ironic tone lets you know he is even more sophisticated than the outsiders. He calls the detective "one of those omniscient and awe-inspiring marvels" in a tone that indicates that the man is anything but awesome. One of the novel's minor villains—in Tom's eyes, at least—is Alfred Temple, another outsider from St. Louis. What

Temple has in common with the two adults is that he *seems* like an adult, dressing like a dandy and wearing shoes. Only one outsider, Becky Thatcher, comes off well. Can you suggest why?

# CHAPTER 25

Twain sets the stage for further adventures with this chapter, in which Tom and Huck hunt for buried treasure. The chapter gives you a wonderful chance to note the many differences between the boys.

Tom can't find anyone to hunt treasure with until he bumps into Huck. Huck goes along, because Tom's proposal promises to be entertaining and free. Huck, you're told, has a "superabundance of that sort of time which is *not* money." Tom is once again the leader of an adventure he designed. Huck regards him as an expert on treasure-hunting, and Tom is happy to live up to Huck's expectations. He explains where treasure is likely to be hidden, who hides it, and why. Huck, whose mind is very practical, can't understand why anyone would hide money. "I'd spend it and have a good time." So would Tom, but he knows from books that "robbers don't do it that way."

NOTE: **"Still-House branch"**   Tom says there may be treasure in the old haunted house "up the Still-House branch." This refers to an actual stream (branch) in Hannibal where one of the town's three distilleries was located.

While digging beneath a dead tree limb, the boys

discuss how they'll spend their treasure. Tom surprises Huck by saying he'll use some of his money to get married. Huck remembers his parents' fights. "The girl I'm going to marry won't fight," Tom says. Is he deceiving himself? How much time have he and Becky spent together without fighting?

The boys haven't dropped their superstitions, as their discussion of witches and ghosts illustrates. Folk wisdom, perhaps gleaned from a book, tells Tom that they can best locate the site of buried treasure at midnight. So the boys return at night—an indication that Tom's fear of Injun Joe has abated. They measure the shadow of a dead limb and start digging. When they find no treasure, they decide they must have measured the shadow at the wrong time.

# CHAPTER 26

The story of Injun Joe speeds up in this chapter. It also picks up some complications—enough to add to the suspense and keep you turning pages.

The next day, the boys meet at the dead tree to collect their tools. They are about to traipse off to a nearby haunted house when Huck remembers that it's Friday—an unlucky day. Huck remembers that the night before he dreamed about rats—a sign, to the superstitious, that the dreamer has secret enemies.

Tom and Huck quickly change their plans. They play Robin Hood all afternoon and return for their tools on Saturday. They smoke and do a little more digging—something that will cause problems later—then head for the haunted house. They are upstairs exploring when two men enter. The boys watch them through the holes in the floor. They recognize one as a deaf and dumb Spaniard who has recently visited the town. But the Spaniard is really Injun Joe, something the boys realize as soon as he speaks.

The two men have planned a "dangerous job," and Injun Joe wants his partner to go "up the river" until the time is right to pull it off. After a lengthy nap, Injun Joe digs a hole in a corner to bury their "swag" (stolen money) in. While digging, his knife strikes a chest full of gold coins. The stranger guesses that the chest was left by a gang led by John A. Murrell (misspelled by Twain as Murrel), an outlaw whose bloody exploits were well known to children growing up along the Mississippi during the 1840s.

With all that money, the stranger suggests that they won't have to do the "job" they'd planned. Injun Joe disagrees. His goal is not just robbery but revenge.

---

**NOTE: Injun Joe's motive**   Revenge is a common motive in this novel. Tom pays Sid back for tattling and vows to avenge Becky's snub. Becky lets Tom get whipped for something he didn't do in order to avenge a deed she expects him to commit. The smaller students take vengeance on Mr. Dobbins by baring his gilded head. And Injun Joe, who murdered Dr. Robinson to avenge an old slight, now plans another vengeful act—one that will be described in Chapter 29.

---

To Tom and Huck's distress, Injun Joe decides not to leave the treasure in the house. Fresh dirt on the boys' tools has made him suspicious. He'll take the booty to his "den": "Number Two—under the cross. The other place [Number One]," he says, "is bad—too common." These clues are not explained further, but you can be sure you'll discover their meaning later on.

---

**NOTE: "By the great Sachem"** Injun Joe swears "by the great Sachem" that he won't rebury the treasure in the house. A sachem was the chief of some American Indian tribes and tribal confederations. In effect, Joe is saying something like, "Good Lord no!" Why might it seem appropriate for Injun Joe to use the word *Sachem* instead of *Lord* or *God*? How might its use suggest that Joe doesn't share the religious values of the people of St. Petersburg?

---

Injun Joe begins to climb the stairs to see if the pick's owner is on the second floor. But the rotten staircase crumbles beneath his weight. Before dark, he and his crony leave the house and head "toward the river" with the treasure.

The boys curse the fact that they brought their dirty tools into the house and made Injun Joe suspicious enough to remove the treasure. They resolve to keep watch out for him and follow him to "Number Two," wherever that might be.

## CHAPTER 27

This brief chapter allows the boys to assess their situation and plot a future course. It also establishes, perhaps more clearly than ever, the differences between Tom, the visionary leader, and Huck, the more down-to-earth follower.

Tom dreams of possessing the treasure but awakens knowing it has eluded his grasp. Thinking how unreal Saturday's adventure seems, he concludes that it might all have been a dream. He rushes out to compare notes with Huck, who assures him that their adventure was painfully real.

Huck is cursing their luck that they failed to get the money. Furthermore, he sees no hope of ever obtaining it, since he believes that a person has "only one chance for such a pile—and that one's lost."

Tom, being more imaginative, is still hopeful. He persuades Huck that they must find Injun Joe and "track the money." Both boys are afraid of confronting Joe, but the lure of money enables them to overcome their fears. Tom guesses that Number Two refers to a room in one of the village's two taverns. In a half hour, he has discovered that room No. 2 in the less expensive tavern is a mystery. The tavern-keeper's son told him it was kept locked all the time and that people use it only at night.

---

**NOTE: Tom's view of Huck**   Notice that Tom investigates the taverns alone because he doesn't "care to have Huck's company in public places." Why do you think he feels this way about Huck? Is Tom a snob? Might he fear getting in trouble by associating with Huck? How might Tom's discomfort with Huck in public show that the residents of St. Petersburg are divided along class lines, and that Tom is very much aware of the class to which he belongs?

---

The boys agree that the mysterious tavern room

is the Number Two they're looking for. The room has an outside entrance whose door Tom hopes he can find a key to. He tells Huck to "get hold of all the door-keys you can find, and I'll nip all of Auntie's." The first dark night, they'll try the keys on the door.

Meanwhile, Tom wants Huck to watch for Injun Joe and follow him if he appears. Huck's not eager to take on this dangerous assignment. But he agrees to do so after Tom reminds him that Joe might pass up a chance to avenge himself and go straight for the money.

Tom turns the meeting into a pep rally at the end. "Don't ever weaken, Huck, and I won't," he says. Is this mere bravado on Tom's part? Or is it an attempt to manipulate Huck—to get him to do something that Tom would rather not do, just as he got his friends to paint his aunt's fence in Chapter 2?

# CHAPTER 28

Tom penetrates room No. 2 and uncovers some secrets not only about Injun Joe but about the hypocrisy of some of St. Petersburg citizens, as well. The chapter gives you another opportunity to study Twain's method of storytelling.

---

NOTE: "That night"   Twain seems to have lost track of time here. Because the episode at the haunted house took place on a Saturday, Chapter 28 must have occurred on a Sunday. Thus, "that night" should mean Sunday night. However, it probably means Monday night. Had he realized the action in Chapter 27 took place on a Sunday, he almost certainly would have mentioned church and perhaps a Bible reading at home after breakfast.

Twain sometimes broke off work on a novel for months or even years before returning to it. Losing track of time is not a major flaw here, unless it confuses you. Nor is it terribly harmful that the summer he describes seems to last at least a month longer than most summers. Still, Twain's carelessness about time is a reminder that when he wrote *The Adventures of Tom Sawyer* he was a novice in the art of novel-writing.

---

The boys keep watch outside the tavern for three nights. On a moonless Thursday night, with thunder rumbling in the distance, Huck stands guard outside the tavern. Tom heads toward the door of No. 2 with his lantern, which he has "blindfolded" with a towel.

Twain doesn't let you follow Tom. Instead, he tries to make you feel Huck's "season of waiting anxiety." How does this approach add to the chapter's suspense?

Suddenly Tom rushes by with his lantern bared and tells Huck to run for his life. The two reach a deserted slaughterhouse just as a storm bursts. There, Tom tells what happened. The door to No. 2 was unlocked. Tom pushed it open and spotted Injun Joe, who was lying dead drunk on the floor. Tom realizes, however, that the room is haunted with spirits other than ghosts.

---

**NOTE: Temperance taverns** Twain takes a second dig at the temperance movement here. During the 1840s, Hannibal had three whiskey distilleries and at least six bars, or "groggeries" as they were called. A temperance tavern was a place where men could assemble without drinking whiskey or beer. Twain is suggesting that even these high-minded places weren't above selling spirits on the sly.

The boys decide it's too risky to return to No. 2 and hunt for the box. Tom figures that the best course is to wait for Injun Joe to leave some night. Huck proves himself less brave than Tom. He offers to do the watching if Tom will do the snatching of the treasure, and Tom agrees. Huck will wake him up if he sees Joe leave.

NOTE: "Good as wheat"   The phrase Huck uses to emphasize his agreement is a comment on their plan. To indicate that the plan is "great," he calls it "good as wheat." The phrase dates back to colonial times, when wheat, a valuable staple food source, was used as a medium of exchange. Something "good as wheat," like something "good as gold," was of solid value.

As the boys leave the slaughterhouse, Huck says he's going to sleep in Ben Rogers' hayloft. This is okay with the Rogers' slave, Uncle Jake, who often shares his food with Huck. Huck and Jake get along because Huck doesn't look down on him.

How might Huck's attitude toward Jake reflect his own situation as an outcast? Why do you think Huck is embarrassed about eating with a slave?

What does Huck's embarrassment tell you about his understanding of acceptable behavior between whites and blacks in a slave state?

# CHAPTER 29

The story of Tom's courtship of Becky overlaps that of Injun Joe's fate in this chapter. And Huck proves himself not only brave but also capable of risking his own neck to help others.

Becky's family has returned to town, and Becky is once more Tom's main interest. Friday, they play games of tag ("hi-spy" and "gully-keeper") with schoolmates, and Becky convinces her mother to let her host a picnic the next day.

The picnic trip begins late Saturday morning. The Thatchers have hired an old steamboat to take the children and their chaperones three miles down the river to eat lunch and frolic. Sid can't go because he is sick, and Mary stays home to care for him. Because the boat is expected to return late, Becky's mother suggests she stay at Susy Harper's house near the ferry landing.

Tom has another plan. He wants to go to the Widow Douglas' house for ice cream after the picnic. He persuades Becky to agree to the plan and tries to forget the fact that Huck might need him.

---

**NOTE: Key details**    Observe throughout this chapter how seemingly insignificant details end up being important to the story. Episodic as Twain's narrative is, it is intricately interrelated. Sid and Mary's absence and Becky's intention to stay at the Harpers' are essential details, as you will see. Introducing the Widow Douglas—by name and reputation—prepares you for action that takes place in the second part of the chapter.

---

The ferryboat lets the children off three miles downstream. They explore McDougal's cave, an enormous, labyrinthine system of chambers too vast for anyone to know completely. Tom has explored it many times before and knows it as well as anyone.

---

NOTE: McDougal's cave   Twain didn't invent this cave. It actually exists south of Hannibal and was called McDowell's cave when Twain was a child. McDowell was a surgeon from St. Louis who once stored weapons there in a plot to invade Mexico. For a number of years he experimented there with the body of a fourteen-year-old said to be his daughter. He stored the body in a copper cylinder filled with alcohol in order to see if the body would turn to stone in the limestone cave.

---

The children split up into groups and reassemble outside the cave at nightfall. The ferry, which has been waiting an hour for its passengers, finally pushes off and moves upstream for home.

Huck is at his post outside the tavern when he sees the ferry go by. Uninvited to the picnic, he wonders for a moment what the boat is. Near midnight, two men leave room No. 2 and brush past him. One is carrying a box that Huck assumes to be the treasure. Despite his fears, he follows the men up Cardiff Hill in hopes of spotting them burying the treasure.

Near the Widow Douglas' house, the men stop. Huck is terrified. He shakes as if taken by "a dozen agues" (fevers).

Injun Joe is upset to find the widow's lights on, because she may have company. Is it Tom and Becky? You won't find out until the next chapter.

Huck realizes that Joe intends to seek revenge on the widow. Although she has been kind to Huck, he doesn't dare call out a warning to her for fear he'll get killed.

Whether she has company or not, Joe intends to get his revenge. The widow's late husband was the judge who jailed him on the vagrancy charges that Dr. Robinson's father brought. Worse, in Joe's eyes, was that the judge had ordered him horse-whipped in public like a slave.

---

**NOTE: A defense of Injun Joe**   Some readers explain Joe's evil as a reaction to racial injustice. They point out that this "half-breed," as Twain identifies him, suffered rejection and public humiliation by the whites of St. Petersburg. This harsh treatment, they argue, made Joe determined to seek revenge from his tormentors. You may reject this interpretation. However, *Tom Sawyer* does reveal Twain's interest in race as a social problem—a major theme in his later novels. Note, for example, the contrast between Joe's treatment by the elder Dr. Robinson and Huck's treatment by Uncle Jake. The white man chased the "half-breed" away from his kitchen while the black man shared his food with the poor white boy. What do you think Twain is saying by making this contrast?

---

Injun Joe doesn't want to kill the widow. He

wants to mutilate her face—"slit her nostrils [and] notch her ears."

Huck holds his breath and slips away. What a wonderfully detailed description Twain gives of Huck's departure. You might want to read it aloud to appreciate how efficiently Twain meshes action and emotion here.

Halfway down the hill, Huck bangs on the Welshman's door. He awakens the old man and his two sons. Notice how careful he is to protect himself. He makes them promise not to reveal the source of their information. In minutes, the three men are up the hill with their guns. Huck hangs back. When the guns go off, he turns and flees down the hill.

---

**NOTE: Huck's maturation**   Is Huck's emerging ability to think beyond his own safety a sign of his growing maturity? Some readers think so. Whether you agree or disagree, you will find support for your view in later chapters.

---

## CHAPTER 30

Twain continues to intertwine the courtship story with Injun Joe's. He moves both stories forward with twists designed to keep St. Petersburg—and you—on edge.

Huck slinks up to the Welshman's door at dawn, hoping to find out what happened at the Widow Douglas's. The Welshman tells him he is "welcome"—the first time Huck can remember anyone saying that to him. Inside, Huck learns that the Welshman's sneeze alerted Injun Joe and the stranger, who escaped despite a chase. A sheriff's posse has waited until daylight to search the woods for the villains.

The Welshman pumps Huck for information about the men. Huck tries hard to oblige without revealing any secrets about the treasure. But his tale has holes in it that make the Welshman suspect that Huck is holding back. Huck startles the Welshman by reporting words spoken by the supposedly mute Spaniard. Caught, Huck admits: " 'Tain't a Spaniard—it's Injun Joe!"

---

NOTE: "White men don't"　The Welshman accepts Huck's revelation immediately because it fits his stereotypical view of Indians as savages. "White men don't take that sort of revenge," he says. Though Twain doesn't tell you how to interpret that remark, some readers think this is being ironic. They argue that his own experience, living during a period of lynchings and civil war, taught him that whites are as capable of mutilating tortures as members of any other race. Why might Twain want to show that a generally decent man like the Welshman harbored warped views of Indians? On the other hand, might Twain, as a member of his society, be capable of sharing the Welshman's views?

---

Twain shifts the scene to church, where Aunt Polly and Mrs. Thatcher are horrified to learn that their children might be lost in the cave. Might they have learned this earlier if Twain hadn't made Sid and Mary stay home, and if he hadn't had Becky's mother ask Becky to stay with the Harpers?

Within five minutes, alarm bells are ringing, and the men of the village are swarming toward the cave. The Cardiff Hill episode is suddenly forgotten. The villagers search the cave for three days and nights and discover only two traces of Becky and Tom: their names written on a wall with candle smoke, and one of Becky's ribbons. Meanwhile, Huck takes sick and is nursed by the Widow Douglas.

---

**NOTE: Huck's illness** Does Huck's illness come on too suddenly for you? It does for many readers, who are reminded that Twain used this device once before, in Chapter 22, when he kept Tom ill for five weeks before the trial began. This time, Twain seems to have a similar problem. He has to keep Huck occupied while you turn your attention to the hunts for Becky and Tom and Injun Joe. What might Twain have had Huck do instead of falling sick?

---

## CHAPTER 31

Though this chapter contains not a grain of humor, many readers think it the most masterfully written in the novel. Twain infuses this misadventure with a nightmarish quality that makes the children's terror yours.

Tom and Becky wander off from their friends and explore the cave alone. Tom ducks behind a limestone "waterfall" and discovers a "natural stairway" into an unexplored section of the cave. Eager to discover new territory, he calls Becky, and they descend into the cave's "secret depths."

Inside an enormous room, the light of their candles excites hundreds of bats, who swoop down at the children. Tom hurries Becky into a corridor just as a bat extinguishes her candle with its wing.

---

**NOTE: Building suspense**  As you read, keep track of the elements that raise your fears for the children's safety. Surely the maze-like caves, where it's easy to get lost, help create the atmosphere of suspense. Next, Twain notes the "vast knots of bats," adding a touch of menace to the adventure merely by mentioning them. Twain then has the bats chase the children and swat out Becky's candle. Suddenly, you are aware of another danger: the vulnerability of the children's source of light. To discover how he controls your emotions, put an X in the margin each time Twain intensifies the suspense by making you aware of a new danger. How might this episode be different if Twain had listed the cave's many dangers in a single paragraph early in the chapter?

---

While avoiding the bats, the children become totally lost. Tom pretends to be confident, but his assurances sound hollow and frighten Becky. Tom's shout returns to him as "a ripple of mocking laughter."

---

**NOTE: Tom's maturity**  Despite moments of despair, Tom manages to keep a cool head throughout this episode and to demonstrate continued emotional growth. He takes the blame for their predicament, then feigns confidence so as not to frighten Becky. He is level-headed enough to seek out a spring and stop there. Watch for more signs of Tom's maturity throughout the chapter.

---

The children share a piece of cake that Becky saved from the picnic. Becky, who yields to her fears more readily than Tom, checks an impulse to call the cake their last meal. They watch their last candle flicker out.

They fall asleep, and when they awaken, Tom figures it must be Tuesday—three days after they entered the cave. Unraveling a kite string as he walks, Tom leads Becky down a corridor and is so startled to see Injun Joe that he shouts. Tom tells Becky, who didn't see Injun Joe, that he shouted only "for luck."

A long while later, back at the spring, Becky gives Tom permission to go exploring alone. She is sure they are doomed and makes him promise to hold her hand when the time comes to die. He kisses her and, with a show of confidence he really doesn't feel, he crawls away on his hands and knees, unraveling the kite line as he goes.

---

**NOTE: A mock marriage?**   Becky and Tom will never be closer than they are here. Their closeness leads some readers to think that in the final part of this chapter, Twain intends to suggest that the children are newlyweds. Becky sets the idea in motion when she speaks of "our wedding cake." The children eat and sleep, then promise to die together—a reminder of the final words of traditional wedding vows: "till death do us part." Finally, Tom shows a protectiveness toward Becky that, at least in literature, is often associated with husbands.

# CHAPTER 32

This chapter provides the climax to the story of Becky and Tom's courtship. Also, Twain begins to resolve many of the novel's remaining questions here.

Late Tuesday afternoon, the scene shifts from the cave to the town. The children are still lost, and the villagers are heartsick. Becky's mother is delirious with grief.

At night, the villagers are aroused from their beds by a "wild peal" of bells—a signal that Becky and Tom have been found. It's the climax of this plot line. The children are paraded through town in an open carriage pulled not by horses but by St. Petersburg citizens. On the "greatest night the little town had ever seen," no one returns to bed. After the parade, a procession of townspeople passes through Becky's house to congratulate and hug the children.

Lying on the couch, Tom fills in the villagers—and you—on the details of their rescue. He followed three corridors the length of his kite line, finally glimpsing a speck of daylight at the end of the third corridor. The exit led to a bluff (cliff) overlooking the Mississippi River. He returned for Becky, who was hard to budge because she had prepared herself mentally for death. Outside, after crying "for gladness," they hailed a rowboat and learned from the two men in it that they were five miles south of the cave entrance.

The men rowed them to a house, fed them, and

made them rest. After dark, they returned to St. Petersburg.

---

**NOTE: Fiction vs. reality**   Twain may have combined three true stories here. In his youth, he and a girl became lost in Hannibal's cave. A search party found them just before their last candle went out. Hannibal's Injun Joe got lost in the cave, too. He managed to survive by eating bats. A town drunk named "General" Gaines was lost in the cave for a week. He "finally pushed his handkerchief out of a hole in a hilltop near Saverton, several miles down the river from the cave's mouth," Twain writes in his *Autobiography*, "and somebody saw it and dug him out."

---

Some townspeople bring Judge Thatcher the good news in the cave, where he and a handful of diehard searchers have been seeking the children. The children are exhausted from their ordeal. Tom stays in bed until Friday; Becky doesn't leave hers until Sunday.

Tom tries to visit Huck on Friday, but his friend is too sick to see him until Monday. Widow Douglas won't let Tom talk about his adventure for fear that it might excite Huck. Tom hears about the Cardiff Hill adventure at home and learns that Injun Joe's sidekick, the "ragged man," was found drowned in the river, where he apparently fell while trying to escape.

Two weeks after his escape from the cave, Tom learns that Judge Thatcher has had the cave sealed with an iron door. Tom is shocked. "Injun Joe's in the cave!" he blurts out.

**NOTE: Tom's reaction**   What does Tom's reaction to the news of the iron door reveal about his character? Although he is frightened to death of the murderer, he seems genuinely upset. The second paragraph of Chapter 33 should give you an insight into Tom's reaction.

# CHAPTER 33

This chapter has two parts: the discovery and disposition of Injun Joe's body and the recovery of the treasure by Huck and Tom. In each part, Twain addresses the story's remaining questions.

Rescuers head for the cave in twelve rowboats, followed by spectators aboard the ferry. What do you make of the fact that Tom rides alongside Judge Thatcher in a rowboat? Has saving Becky's life brought him to the top of St. Petersburg society?

The discovery of Injun Joe lying dead inside the cave door is the climax of the plot line that tracks his fate. Tom has mixed feelings about the "sorrowful sight." He pities Joe because he imagines how much the trapped man suffered. However, Joe's corpse affords him an immense sense of relief, much as he felt it would back in Chapter 24. You may remember that the idea that Joe might be captured alive frightened Tom, who thought he would feel safe only after viewing Joe's corpse.

Joe had survived by eating bats and candle wax and drinking water that dripped into a cup scooped into the stump of a stalagmite (a deposit of calcium carbonate on the floor of a cave). The drip— amounting to a spoonful every day—prompts Twain to meditate on the possibility that natural laws, not chance, govern all events. "Has everything a purpose and a mission?" he asks. "Did this drop fall patiently during five thousand years to be ready for this flitting human insect's need?"

---

**NOTE: Determinism**   What does this speculation have to do with the progress of the story or with the interests of Twain's primarily juvenile audience? Very little, it would seem, although it has everything to do with Twain's budding interest in determinist philosophy. In later years, Twain would become fascinated with the doctrine of determinism, which holds that all events have causes and that free will is an illusion. How might the superstitions that Twain sprinkles through *Tom Sawyer* also indicate his interest in determinism?

---

Injun Joe's funeral is well attended, both by people who would have preferred him hanged and by those who had been eager to petition the governor for his pardon. Twain reserves special disdain for those who wanted the murderer pardoned. "If he had been Satan himself," Twain says, "plenty of weaklings would have signed a petition to save him."

---

**NOTE: Twain's reaction to insincerity**   This satirical swipe lacks the gentleness of much of Twain's humor. Does it strike you, as it does some readers, as overly harsh? Compare its tone with those of Chapter 24, when he satirizes the detective from St. Louis, or Chapter 12, when he mocks Aunt Polly's experiments with Pain-Killer. How is Twain's humor gentler in these cases than here?

---

The day after the funeral, Tom takes Huck aside and tells him he's sure that the treasure is in the cave. Huck's not sure he has the strength to hunt for it, so Tom offers to row him down and back. This time, Tom is prepared for the cave's perils. The boys assemble bags, pipes, extra kite strings, and "lucifer matches"—wood matches with phosphorous tips that were "new-fangled" in the 1840s.

The boys "borrow" a rowboat and float down to the hole through which Becky and Tom escaped the cave. The hole is so well hidden, Tom has decided to use it as a hideout when he becomes a robber. Once more, he becomes Huck's teacher, explaining the attractions of the robber's life.

Deep inside the cave, the boys come to the corner where Tom had seen Injun Joe. He points out a cross marked on a big rock with candle smoke. The boys explore around the rock and locate the box of gold coins.

Tom and Huck carry the money out of the cave in bags, and Tom rows them back to St. Petersburg. There they decide to hide the money in the Widow Douglas' woodshed. They "borrow" a child's wagon to haul their treasure up Cardiff Hill where they meet Mr. Jones, the Welshman. Mr. Jones tells them that people are waiting for them at the Widow Douglas'. He doesn't say why as he helps them pull the wagon, which he thinks holds scrap metal.

At Mrs. Douglas', he pushes the boys into the drawing room. All of the village's important people are there: the minister, the editor, the Thatchers, and Aunt Polly, among others. The boys are filthy. Mrs. Douglas takes them into a bedroom and gives them new clothes to put on.

What's the purpose of the gathering? Twain

doesn't tell you, in order to entice you to turn the page.

## CHAPTER 34

Huck is welcomed into the fold of St. Petersburg society—something he's not quite ready for. Twain draws a further contrast between the two boys, showing once more how Huck and Tom differ.

Tom and Huck are dressing as the chapter opens. Huck can think only of escape—of "sloping" (slipping away) by letting themselves down to the ground with a rope. Tom, who wants to stay, won't hear of it.

Sid enters the room and explains that the party is to thank the Welshman and his sons for protecting the widow. Sid also knows that the Welshman plans to surprise the gathering by revealing Huck's part in protecting the widow. Yet Sid has spoiled the plan by giving away the secret beforehand. Angry that Sid would sink so low, Tom kicks him out of the room and dares him to tattle.

At supper downstairs, Mr. Jones makes his announcement about Huck, and the guests pretend to be surprised. Huck shrinks from the attention, which makes him want to crawl under a rock. Why do you think he responds to praise so differently than Tom?

Tom sees his chance to jump into the spotlight when the widow says she'll house and educate Huck and someday give him money to start a business. "Huck don't need it," Tom says. "Huck's rich!" The guests think he's making a joke. Tom rushes outside and returns with the sacks of coins, which he spills on the table. When it's counted, it amounts to more than $12,000—a sum larger than anyone has ever seen at one time.

# CHAPTER 35

The book's final chapter gives you a glimpse of Tom and Huck's life after they've achieved "success." As you read, watch how their characters remain consistent to the end.

Tom and Huck's newfound wealth has changed not just their lives but the lives of everyone in the village. Even "grave, unromantic men" are ransacking abandoned houses, board by board, in hopes of finding stashed treasure.

The boys have become celebrities, "courted, admired, stared at" everywhere. They are quoted and written about, and their pasts are "discovered to bear marks of conspicuous originality."

---

**NOTE: Creating a myth**   Twain calls the boys' $12,000 a "windfall," something that came their way by luck. But the townspeople refuse to accept that explanation. Instead, they create a myth about Tom and Huck, emphasizing episodes in their pasts to explain how the boys obtained the treasure as a result of their cleverness. Suddenly, almost against their wills, Tom and Huck have become model boys. Why does Twain make fun of this effort to misunderstand the boys' success? How is his description of Tom and Huck's treatment part of his parody of the "good-boy" books he so detested?

---

Tom and Huck have hefty incomes now: about $360 a year each, more than the minister can hope to earn. It's an enormous sum at a time when, as Twain tells you, a boy cost his parents only about $65 a year to house, clothe, feed, and educate. No wonder they have become celebrities!

Judge Thatcher, who once heard Tom flub a question on Jesus' disciples, now thinks Tom an extraordinary boy. He hopes to see Tom attend West Point and law school.

Huck, however, can't stand his new life. He disappears from Mrs. Douglas' house after suffering through three weeks of cleanliness, good manners, and other "bars and shackles of civilization." Tom finds him, ragged once more, in an empty hogshead down by the slaughterhouse. "Everything's so awful reglar," Huck says about the widow's household, "a body can't stand it." To rid himself of all the headaches involved with wealth, he offers his money to Tom.

Tom refuses the money and tricks Huck into giving his new life another chance. "Being rich ain't going to keep me back from turning robber," he says. For Huck to be part of the gang, however, he must be respectable. Being a robber isn't like being a pirate, Tom explains. "A robber is more high-toned." Convinced, Huck agrees to try the widow's house for another month.

---

**NOTE: Perils of wealth**  Twain makes some interesting points about wealth and wealthy people. "Being rich ain't what it's cracked up to be," Huck says. It's "a-wishing you was dead all the time." Twain satirizes the wealthy, too, by suggesting that they are less than honest. "In most countries," Tom says, "[robbers are] awful high up in the nobility— dukes and such." Remember that Twain co-authored an attack on corruption in high places in *The Gilded Age*.

---

As the novel ends, the boys are lost in a fantasy

about their gang of robbers. Complete with initiation ceremonies and secret pledges signed in blood, the gang sounds like a club. But the boys don't notice this. Huck even believes the widow will be proud of him if he succeeds at robbery.

Can a boy with these beliefs ever be civilized? To find out, you'll have to read *The Adventures of Huckleberry Finn*, where Twain retells the final chapter of *Tom Sawyer* on the first page.

---

**NOTE: Selling out—or remaining true?** In this chapter, Tom becomes a spokesman for the society whose rules he tested throughout the novel. Is this turn of events out of character? Is it a sign of his maturity? Does it make Tom a traitor to the "cause" of boyhood—one Huck still represents with his refusal to live within civilization's bounds?

The way you answer these questions will depend on your perception of Tom's character. Many readers hold that he is a part of St. Petersburg's mainstream from the start, unlike outcasts such as Huck, Injun Joe, and Uncle Jake. Far from rebelling against this society, these readers argue, Tom tries hard to win its respect and to dominate it by engaging others in his fantasies. What evidence does the novel contain, if any, that might enable you to contradict this argument?

---

## CONCLUSION

Twain ends *The Adventures of Tom Sawyer* with two paragraphs that make a joke out of stopping the story. He claims that he ended the novel to keep it from becoming the story of a man. Moreover, he indicates that ending novels about juveniles is an uncertain procedure for which there are few guidelines. Novelists who write about adults have an easier time, he suggests, because their stories invariably end with marriages.

The second paragraph continues to promote the idea, mentioned in the Preface, that the novel is largely factual. "Most of the characters that perform in this book still live," Twain says. He states that he might tell the story of their adult lives later.

Twain uses the word "perform" to describe what the book's characters do. How might this word be a key to understanding the characters and their perceptions of themselves as actors on public display?

# A STEP BEYOND

# Tests and Answers

## TESTS

### Test 1

1. A major theme of *Tom Sawyer* can be stated _____
   as:
   - I. "There's more than one road to success."
   - II. "Boys will be boys."
   - III. "Nice guys finish last."
   - A. I, II, and III      B. I and II only
   - C. II and III only

2. Sunday school gives most of the children _____
   and adults present a chance to
   - A. swap stories      B. show off
   - C. plan the week's events

3. Tom is drawn to Huck in part because _____
   - A. Huck is more imaginative than Tom
   - B. Tom enjoys Huck's sense of humor
   - C. Tom has been forbidden to play with Huck

4. Tom's courtship of Becky burlesques _____
   - A. children pretending to be grown up
   - B. divisions of labor by gender
   - C. adult courtship

5. Showing off is a St. Petersburg pastime that _____
   - A. only Tom engages in

    B. only Tom and other children engage in

    C. both adults and children engage in

6. Tom's pangs of conscience can be traced to _____
    A. his inborn sense of right and wrong
    B. the harsh teachings of his church
    C. his poor self-image

7. The superstitions mentioned throughout the _____
novel
    A. suggest the primitive nature of the
       children's minds
    B. add to the realism of Twain's portrait
       of small-town life
    C. both A and B

8. After discovering they had been tricked into _____
a funeral for three boys who were still alive,
the villagers are
    A. enraged
    B. grateful for the entertainment
    C. awed by the originality of the trick

9. Tom finally wins Becky's heart by _____
    A. kissing her
    B. rescuing her from the cave
    C. taking her whipping

10. The narrator's anger is most easily excited _____
by
    A. signs of insincerity
    B. people motivated by revenge
    C. the villagers' vanity

11. In what way is *Tom Sawyer* an idyll—a work of literature that paints country life as a scene of tranquil
happiness?

12. In his *Autobiography*, Twain notes that in his home-
    town of Hannibal "there were grades of society . . .
    class lines were quite clearly drawn." Point out some
    of the class divisions in St. Petersburg, and show
    how they help shape the villagers' attitudes and ac-
    tions.

13. Contrast Tom's character with Huck's, noting how
    each is the other's foil—someone who brings out
    another's character more sharply.

14. Discuss the novel's four main story lines as illustra-
    tions of Tom's growth. How does each demonstrate
    his movement toward maturity?

# Test 2

1. Throughout the novel, Tom's major goal    \_\_\_\_\_
   is to
   A. please Polly
   B. be the center of attention
   C. impress Becky Thatcher

2. Injun Joe is mainly motivated by          \_\_\_\_\_
   A. greed
   B. confusion over his ancestry
   C. revenge

3. Polly goes against her religious beliefs—her    \_\_\_\_\_
   "duty"—by
   A. quoting Scripture
   B. blaming Tom for breaking the sugar
      bowl
   C. not punishing Tom severely

4. Tom runs away to Jackson's Island    \_\_\_\_\_
   because he
   A. feels sorry for himself

    B.  wants to attend his own funeral
    C.  likes to camp out

5. Tom hurts Polly's feelings when he    \_\_\_\_\_
    A.  attends his funeral
    B.  lets her think he is a clairvoyant
    C.  feeds the cat Pain-Killer

6. Tom's membership in the Cadets of Tem-    \_\_\_\_\_
    perance and the discovery of whiskey in
    the Temperance Tavern give Twain a chance
    to
    A.  satirize hypocrisy
    B.  show the harm of bad habits
    C.  support the cause of temperance

7. At first, Huck doesn't tell the Welshman    \_\_\_\_\_
    who the "Spaniard" is because he
    A.  wants credit for capturing Injun Joe
    B.  doesn't know who he is
    C.  is afraid of reprisal from Injun Joe

8. Tom discovers an exit from the cave during    \_\_\_\_\_
    A.  daylight hours
    B.  the hours of darkness
    C.  a thunderstorm

9. The villagers refuse to believe that Tom and    \_\_\_\_\_
    Huck's good fortune came their way
    A.  mostly by accident
    B.  through the boys' cleverness
    C.  honestly

10. Tom persuades Huck to return to the wid-    \_\_\_\_\_
    ow's house by telling him that if he does,
    he can
    A.  go to West Point and law school

   B.  join Tom's gang of robbers

   C.  eat well and wear clean clothes

11. In what ways is *Tom Sawyer* a satire of people's desires for power and money?

12. Discuss Tom's uncanny ability to turn nearly everything into play.

13. Twain had a fondness for burlesques—takeoffs on literary conventions and forms. What are the targets of his burlesques in *Tom Sawyer*, and how does he make fun of his targets?

14. What role does religion play in the novel and in the lives of the people of St. Petersburg?

# ANSWERS

## Test 1

1. B    2. B    3. C    4. C    5. C    6. B
7. C    8. B    9. C   10. A

11. An idyll is a composition in poetry or prose that paints a scene or episode, especially in country life, as one of tranquil happiness. Twain's portrait of St. Petersburg—the Hannibal of his youth—is very much an idyll, painted by a man looking back to his childhood across the span of thirty years. The first paragraph of Chapter 2 sets the stage for such a portrait, describing "the summer world . . . a song in every heart . . . a Delectable Land" of Cardiff Hill. Another day opens in Chapter 4 with the sun rising "upon a tranquil world."

Tragedies and near-tragedies do occur in this idyll, of course: a murder, a framing, a death by starvation, a drowning, the near death of Becky and Tom and the attempted disfigurement of Mrs. Douglas. However, Twain's treatment of these episodes takes the threat and the horror out of them.

Vanity and vindictiveness exist in St. Petersburg, but they are presented with indulgence—with a wink that renders them harmless. Tom lies, cheats, shows off, fights, and steals. But the narrator's tolerant attitude—boys, after all, will be boys—places these acts in a neutral moral zone. Despite the violence and the genuinely terrifying moments in the cave, all ends happily, with the town in peace—surely an idyllic ending.

**12.** Though Twain doesn't focus on it, a class system does exist in St. Petersburg, and it determines the villagers' attitudes toward one another. At the top of the social ladder are such notables as Mrs. Douglas and Judge Thatcher. At the bottom are the outcasts: Injun Joe, the half-breed; Jim and Uncle Jake, slaves; and Muff Potter and Huckleberry Finn, who sleep and eat wherever they can. Tom Sawyer, who has two sets of clothes, is somewhere in between: a member of St. Petersburg's poor but respectable middle class.

Class determines attitude in St. Petersburg. Respectable parents forbid their children to associate with Huck Finn. Most, like Polly and Mrs. Douglas, keep slaves. Injun Joe is scorned and turned away from Dr. Robinson's door. In Chapter 27, Tom admits he "does not care to have Huck's company in public places."

There's a hierarchy even among the outcasts. The slaves are at the bottom of the bottom. Huck is embarrassed to say he ate with Uncle Jake. Joe is irate that he was whipped "like a nigger."

It is possible to move from rung to rung on St. Petersburg's social ladder. Through courage and imagination, Tom raises himself to the top, winning Becky's heart and her parents' approval. Huck's share of the treasure raises him a couple of notches, against his will. In St. Petersburg, money and celebrity bring status, and in the end, the boys have a great deal of all three.

**13.** Tom is educated, romantic, and imaginative. Huck is uneducated and matter-of-fact, and although he enjoys playing pirate and robber—romantic pursuits to a boy—he is not imaginative enough to think these games up by himself. When Tom and Joe invite Huck to become a pirate, "he joined them promptly, for all careers were one to him; he was indifferent."

Huck defers to Tom's superior knowledge of piracy, treasure-hunting, and robbers. In this he is Tom's foil, reminding you of the distance between the two in social class and education. In Chapter 10, Huck is "filled with admiration" for Tom's writing ability. In Chapter 35, he falls for Tom's ploy about the need for Huck to be respectable if he is to join Tom Sawyer's gang.

Tom is the leader, Huck the follower. Each acts as a foil for the other, showing, by contrast, the ways each boy's character differs from the other's. These contrasts extend to their maturity. In some ways, Huck is more "worldly" and experienced than the civilized Tom. Huck teaches Tom to smoke—making him sick. In addition, Huck's independence is a reminder, to you and to Tom, of just how constrained by civilization the rest of St. Petersburg's citizens are.

**14.** Tom moves from childishness to maturity in each of the four story lines. He begins his courtship of Becky by showing off "in all sorts of absurd boyish ways in order to win her admiration" (Chapter 3). Later, he takes her whipping (Chapter 20) and rescues her from the cave (Chapter 32). The Muff Potter episode begins with a superstitious trip to the graveyard (Chapter 9) and ends with Tom's courageous appearance in court (Chapter 23). The Jackson's Island story begins with Tom's feeling sorry for himself (Chapter 13); it ends with his apology to Polly for his "mean and shabby" joke (Chapter 19). Tom and Huck's aimless digging for treasure

(Chapter 25) starts them on the way to solving the mystery of Injun Joe's disappearance. By the end of that story (Chapter 35), Tom has become a spokesman, to Huck, for the ways of civilization.

## Test 2
**1.** B  **2.** C  **3.** C  **4.** A  **5.** B  **6.** A
**7.** C  **8.** A  **9.** A  **10.** B

**11.** Twain pokes fun at people's lust for power and money throughout the novel. Some readers see the whitewashing episode in Chapter 2 as a satire on the society's acquisitiveness. Tom wheels and deals, manipulating others for his own gain. But all Tom's capitalistic enterprise is essentially futile. His "wealth" is a laughable collection of odds and ends. He trades these items for tickets that earn him a cheap Bible. But he doesn't want the Bible; he wants the glory that comes from winning the Bible. Some readers believe this is Twain's sly way of poking fun at the urge to own "things"—which turn out, in the end, not to be worth owning at all.

In Chapter 35, Twain mocks the "grave, unromantic men" who turn into children, seeking treasure in every haunted house in the county. Huck's disappointment with being rich all the time" makes their quest look doubly ridiculous. Finally, Tom deflates the notion that people of money and stature are necessarily better than anyone else, when he tells Huck that in many countries robbers are part of the nobility.

In similar ways, Twain cuts the people of power in Tom's world down to size. Judge Thatcher is revered because "he had traveled, and seen the world"—Constantinople, twelve miles away. Mr. Dobbins, a visiting detective, the superintendent of the Sunday school, and the Rev. Mr. Sprague—all are made less than impressive by Twain's portraits of them. Twain seems to be saying that the powerful are no better than the rest of us, and probably worse.

**12.** Tom has a wonderful knack for turning nearly everything into play—and for getting others to play with him. You can find examples of this knack in nearly every episode. Work becomes play—for himself and his chums—in the whitewashing scene (Chapter 3); church becomes play—for himself and other churchgoers—in Chapter 5; medical treatment becomes "play"—for himself and a cat—in Chapter 12; his self-pity becomes an adventure on Jackson's Island; and his "death" becomes an entertainment for the entire town (Chapter 17). You can add innumerable examples to this list.

**13.** The major targets of Twain's burlesques are juvenile literature which claims that only virtue and industry are rewarded; prayers, sermons, and eulogies; literary compositions encouraged by schools; and adult courtship. The entire novel turns the good-boy stories on their heads, showing that bad (i.e., mischievous) boys can become rich, famous, and respected. Tom is the exact opposite of the model boy. While it's hard to demonstrate that he owes his success to his mischievousness, it's certainly true that he succeeds in spite of it.

Twain burlesques church services in Chapter 5 and pokes fun at the insincerity of eulogies in Chapter 17. In Chapter 5, Twain skewers everything from the minister's reading of notices to the irrelevantly detailed prayer and the absurd sermon that "thinned the predestined elect down to a company so small as to be hardly worth the saving." The minister's eulogy at the funeral paints pictures of boys that the villagers never knew—and yet everyone accepts his "whitewashing" of the boys' misdeeds as the true interpretation.

Twain mocks the "petted melancholy," the "fine language," and the phony sermonizing of school compositions in Chapter 21. Reread that chapter for examples.

He makes gentle fun of the conventions of courtship by having children "act out" the ups and downs of adult relationships. Tom and Becky flirt, show off, quarrel, sulk, and demonstrate just how childish many of the elements of adult courtship are.

**14.** Religion plays an important role in the lives of the villagers and as a device for moving the novel's action forward. The church is a focus of village social life—a form of entertainment. (See Chapters 4, 5, 17, and 30.) But it is also a powerful tool of social control. Religion preached in St. Petersburg holds out the prospect of "fire and brimstone," or hell, to sinners. This prospect makes Tom, Polly, and many others painfully aware of their shortcomings. Note Joe Harper and Tom at the end of Chapter 13, saying their prayers "lest they might call down a sudden and special thunderbolt from Heaven." Because the Bible teaches them not to steal, they feel guilty about having stolen the provisions they brought to the island, and their guilt won't let them sleep.

Polly also looks to religion as a guide to disciplining Tom. She thinks that the Bible says, "Spare the rod and spoil the child" (it doesn't). To keep her conscience from rebelling—and to follow what she thinks is a religious injunction—she punishes Tom by making him whitewash the fence. In this way, her fear of God plays a role in moving the story forward.

Tom's "harassed conscience," also attributable to his religious beliefs, forces him to the witness stand in Muff Potter's defense. His testimony ends one story line while triggering the start of another—that of Injun Joe's fate and the treasure.

# Term Paper Ideas and other Topics for Writing

## Characters

**1.** Choose any four of Tom's adventures and show how they express his character—for example, his inventiveness, his romantic nature, his drive to be the center of attention.

**2.** Show how the different backgrounds of Tom and Huck might have contributed to their contrasting characters.

**3.** Explain how Becky Thatcher's behavior makes her no more of a "model girl" than Tom is a "model boy."

**4.** How might Injun Joe's actions be explained as the result of racial injustice?

## Setting

**1.** In what ways is *Tom Sawyer* a portrait of a small-town society?

**2.** How does Twain exploit the setting to develop characters and adventures?

**3.** In your view, does St. Petersburg live up to its name—as a heavenly place?

## Literary Topics

**1.** "Satire," says the English writer Ian Jack, "is born of the instinct to protest; it is protest become art." In what way does *Tom Sawyer* fit Jack's definition of satire?

**2.** Discuss the first two paragraphs of Chapter 14 and the storm scene in Chapter 16 as examples of Twain's ability to describe nature.

**3.** Discuss Twain's criticism of the compositions read on Examination Night in Chapter 21.

## Themes

**1.** Discuss the roles of vanity and revenge in *Tom Sawyer*.

**2.** Discuss *Tom Sawyer* as an exploration of the conflict between adults and children.

**3.** Show how death—either real, imagined, or threatened—is present throughout *Tom Sawyer*.

## Miscellaneous

**1.** Analyze the sources of Tom's leadership ability.

**2.** How do the superstitions recorded in the novel contribute to the plot and characterizations?

**3.** Explain how *Tom Sawyer* appeals to nostalgia—the longing for the past.

**4.** How would you account for *Tom Sawyer's* appeal to people of all ages and all nationalities?

# Further Reading
## CRITICAL WORKS

Blair, Walter. *Mark Twain & Huck Finn*. Berkeley and Los Angeles: University of California Press, 1960. Fine study of the sources of Twain's characters and art.

———"On the Structure of *Tom Sawyer*," *Modern Philology* 37, No. 1 (August 1939). Key analysis.

Cox, James M. *Mark Twain: The Fate of Humor*. Princeton: Princeton University Press, 1966. Explores Twain's contribution to American humor.

DeVoto, Bernard. *Mark Twain at Work*. Cambridge, Massachusetts: Harvard University Press, 1942. Explains Twain's method of composition.

Elliott, George P. "Afterword," *The Adventures of Tom Sawyer*. New York: Signet/New American Library, 1959. A view by a critic who finds the novel lightweight.

Geismar, Maxwell. *Mark Twain: An American Prophet*. New York: McGraw-Hill, 1970. An admiring critical portrait of Twain as a revolutionary spirit.

Kaplan, Justin. *Mr. Clemens and Mark Twain: A Biography*. New York: Simon & Schuster, 1966. Explores the way Twain fashioned a "second identity" from his thirties until his death.

Kazin, Alfred. "Afterword," *The Adventures of Tom Sawyer*. New York: Bantam, 1981. Discusses the way Twain's memories of boyhood were "touched with dread."

Miller, Robert Keith. *Mark Twain*. New York: Frederick Ungar, 1983. Excellent introduction to Twain's life and work, synthesizes most recent Twain scholarship.

Rogers, Franklin R. *Mark Twain's Burlesque Patterns*. Dallas: Southern Methodist University Press, 1960. A study of Twain's takeoffs on literary conventions.

Stone, Albert E., Jr. *The Innocent Eye*. New Haven: Yale University Press, 1961. Twain's use of "innocent" narrators and protagonists as a means of exposing folly.

Wecter, Dixon. *Sam Clemens of Hannibal*. Boston: Houghton Mifflin, 1952. A study of Twain's roots.

Wiggins, Robert A. *Mark Twain, Jackleg Novelist*. Seattle: University of Washington Press, 1964. Twain and the frontier tradition.

# AUTHOR'S OTHER WORKS

## Novels

| 1873 | *The Gilded Age* (with Charles Dudley Warner) |
| 1882 | *The Prince and the Pauper* |
| 1884 | *The Adventures of Huckleberry Finn* |

1889    *A Connecticut Yankee in King Arthur's Court*
1892    *The American Claimant* (with William Dean Howells)
1894    *The Tragedy of Pudd'nhead Wilson and the Comedy of Those Extraordinary Twins*
1896    *Personal Recollections of Joan of Arc*
1894    *Tom Sawyer Abroad*
1896    *Tom Sawyer, Detective*
1916    *The Mysterious Stranger*

## Nonfiction
1869    *The Innocents Abroad*
1872    *Roughing It*
1880    *A Tramp Abroad*
1883    *Life on the Mississippi*
1897    *Following the Equator*
1897    *How to Tell a Story and Other Essays*
1906    *What Is Man?*
1907    *Christian Science*
1907    *Captain Stormfield's Visit to Heaven*
1959    *The Autobiography of Mark Twain* (Charles Neider, ed.)

## Stories and Sketches
1867    *The Celebrated Jumping Frog of Calaveras County, and Other Sketches*
1875    *Sketches, New and Old*
1876    "The Facts Concerning the Recent Carnival of Crime in Connecticut"
1882    "The Stolen White Elephant"
1891    "Luck"
1893    "The £1,000,000 Bank Note"
1899    "The Man That Corrupted Hadleyburg"
1902    "The Five Boons of Life"
1902    "Was It Heaven? Or Hell?"

# The Critics

## Tom's Immaturity

. . . If Tom is "hampered" as well as harassed, it is because he is incapable of learning from experience. He may be successful at the end of his adventures—in terms of fortune and social status. But he is not a whit the wiser. Although some critics hold that *The Adventures of Tom Sawyer* chronicles Tom's progress from childhood to maturity, the evidence suggests otherwise. One might expect his experience at Muff Potter's trial to have been at least a little sobering, but afterward Tom still likes to play at being a robber. He is later given much credit for leading Becky out of the cave, but it should be remembered that he is responsible for getting them lost in the first place. After making it back to safety, he reveals that his juvenile egotism remains intact. When he tells others about this adventure, he puts in "many striking additions to adorn it withal."

—Robert Keith Miller, *Mark Twain*, 1983

## Comedy of Evil

What is apparent in the blissful atmosphere of frontier boyhood in *Tom Sawyer* is that the sense of evil is comic too. The 'diabolism' of the hero . . . is itself a form of playful parody; and life is basically innocent and loving. If *Tom Sawyer* is, on one level, a parody of an adult society of power and manipulation, of property and place, of trading and acquisition—the parody itself is divine, is innocent, is wistful and comic. (That is the real secret of the book's lasting appeal.) Beneath all the humor is the deeper rhythm of Sam Clemens' affinity with animal life and a natural sense of pleasure.

—Maxwell Geismar, *Mark Twain, an American Prophet*, 1970

## The World As Play

Tom's play *defines the world as play*, and his reality lies in his commitment to play, not in the involuntary tendencies which are often attributed to him.

Actually Tom is in revolt against nothing. To be sure, he feels the pinch of school and the discipline of Aunt Polly, but he has no sustained desire to escape and no program of rebellion. What he does have is a perennial dream of himself as the hero and a commitment to the dream which makes it come true not once, but as many times as he can reorganize the village around his dream. The truth the dream invariably comes to is *play*—a play which converts all serious projects in the town to pleasure and at the same time subverts all the adult rituals by revealing that actually they are nothing but dull play to begin with.

—James M. Cox, *Mark Twain:*
*The Fate of Humor*, 1966

## St. Petersburg's Social History

The items of Twain's social history of St. Petersburg make an impressive tally: a Sunday School exercise, a church service, the village school, an informal inquest, a funeral, "Examination Day," a murder trial, a manhunt, and a reception. Senator Benton's Fourth of July speech disappoints Tom, as does the revival, but the circus does not. The inclusiveness of the catalogue may go unnoted simply because each event is presented as part of Tom's daily life. Always the dramatic focus, his personality unfolds as these manifold social forces act upon him. Tom Sawyer is, for all his imagination, essentially a passive character. True to the observed nature of childhood, Twain has made his hero, in spite of occasional smashing victories over adults, subservient in the main to the adult schedule of events.

—Albert E. Stone, Jr., *The Innocent*
*Eye: Childhood in Mark Twain's*
*Imagination*, 1961